SNOW JOB

SNOW JOB:

Canada, the United States and Vietnam (1954 to 1973)

Charles Taylor

Anansi/Toronto

Published with the assistance of the Canada Council
and the Ontario Council of the Arts.

Cover design by Lynn Campbell
Cover photo by World Wide Photo
Photograph by Alex MacDonald

House of Anansi Press Limited
Toronto Canada

Library of Congress Card Number: 74-77028
ISBN: 0-88784-619-X Paper
       0-88784-717-X Cloth

Printed and bound in Canada by The Hunter Rose Company

74   75   76   77   78   5   4   3   2   1

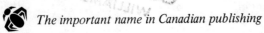 *The important name in Canadian publishing*

To Marina

In a bad time, people, from an outpost of empire I write
bewildered, though on about living. It is to set down a nation's
failure of nerve; I mean complicity . . .

The humiliations of imperial necessity
are an old story, though it does not
improve in the telling and no man
believes it of himself.
Why bring up genocide? Why bring up
acquiescence, profiteering? . . . Doesn't the
service of quiet diplomacy require dirty hands?

Dennis Lee
Civil Elegies

INTRODUCTION

Nations, like individuals, live by myths. These myths may be unconscious or only dimly perceived but they provide the foundation for our actions and opinions; however subtly or imprecisely they condition and shape our view of our place in the world. Yet myths are not historical truths; they are often strongest and most pervasive when based upon distortion and self-deception. There is always an element of wishful feeling.

With some nations there is little difficulty in identifying the basic myths. Consider the United States, Russia, China, France, Great Britain: each has a pattern of behaviour, established over centuries, which reveals the clear outline of collective beliefs, which survives and transcends mere political change, however revolutionary, and which explains most major diplomatic and military actions, however odious. It is not even necessary for a nation to have a long and glorious history or an excess of worldly power: we can clearly perceive the impulses which animate the policies of a Sweden, an Israel or a Tanzania.

Not so with Canada. While Canadians have become more assured in articulating a sense of national identity, we still find it difficult to establish what Canada should *mean* in world affairs. Our brief history is full of potent myths but these offer little guidance for our behaviour beyond our borders. To anticipate the argument, a handful of Mounties riding into the camp of Sitting Bull may or may not be worthy national heroes; they are certainly dangerous exemplars for a Canadian officer in the jungles of Vietnam.

i

Diffidence and self-depreciation have long been among our most striking characteristics as a people; they are also a bad foundation for myth-making. Compare them to the effortless ease with which the Chinese and the French convey their deep convictions of cultural superiority or the sweeping arrogance with which the Americans (and, before them, the British) have justified their imperial schemes: such assertive and often aggressive philosophies are foreign to the Canadian experience and the Canadian character. As Hugh MacLennan has pointed out,[1] the four ethnic groups that came together to create Confederation — the French, the Loyalists, the Scots and the Irish — were the children of separate defeats and abandonments. This helps to explain their strange lack of conviction about their new national identity and their fear of proclaiming total loyalty to the land in which they lived. Such survivors — and their descendants — could only look beyond their borders with doubt and hesitation.

Nevertheless, certain myths did develop in the aftermath of World War Two, from which Canada had emerged relatively unscathed with a burgeoning industry, an élite of skilled civil servants and an influence that was out of all proportion to its population. Canadians gained confidence and pride as their statesmen made major contributions to the establishment of the United Nations and other international institutions and played a key part in turning the British Empire into a multi-racial Commonwealth. Almost as striking were Canada's role in NATO and NORAD and its contribution to the UN side in the Korean War. For about a decade it seemed that we really mattered in the world.

Out of these achievements Canadians evolved certain ideas about their international behavior, certain myths that were partly a matter of style and partly a matter of substance. Under the Liberal governments of Louis St Laurent and Lester Pearson — and to a much lesser extent when John Diefenbaker and the Conservatives were in power — these ideas shaped our policies in a rapidly changing international community in which Canada's influence was steadily diminished, Cold War certainties began to crumble and a proliferation of new states in the developing world posed a multitude of challenges.

There are two major myths which sustained Canadian foreign policy during the 1950s and 1960s and which have survived — partly discredited but still powerful — into the 1970s. These are the myths of Quiet Diplomacy and Canada-as-Helpful-Fixer. Both have the same rationale: Canada has influence in the world because it is a loyal member of the Western alliance *and* a good friend of the developing nations. With neither a colonizing past to overcome, nor an imperialistic present to dissemble, with tireless diplomats and an abundant store of selfless common sense, Canada can be trusted by nearly everyone. But — and this is the hooker — Canadian statesmen will only be effective if they speak softly while they carry their slim dispatch cases from capital to capital, from crisis to crisis. To be outspoken — especially against the United States — might gratify Canadian public opinion, but it would also destroy our effectiveness in Washington and hence damage our credibility elsewhere.

It is easy to see how these ideas relate to certain national characteristics. They confirm our rather smug and self-satisfied view of ourselves: good guys who don't mean harm to anyone. Helpful Fixing implies an attractive idealism, while a quiet diplomat is the logical envoy of a diffident people. There is also an implicit desire to be *liked* by everyone; it seems a natural instinct for a nation built precariously on defeat, abandonment and exile.

Yet Canadians are seldom entirely happy in their diffidence. From the depths of our national psyche there emerges on occasion a contrary impulse which is raw and strident and self-righteous. Often to the detriment of our diplomacy it makes us pompous and pontifical. These holier-than-thou

iii

periods are exceptional but they cause wonder and dismay among our friends. They are the mirror-image of the Quiet Diplomacy which usually emanates from Ottawa as well as a reminder that Canadians as a nation still lack assurance and mature self-confidence.

There is no call for cynicism, only a careful reappraisal. In the 1950s and 1960s, Canadian diplomacy achieved notable triumphs which gave strong credence to the myths of Quiet Diplomacy and Helpful Fixing. Pearson's mediation in the Suez war of 1956 is the best-known example; successive Canadian leaders from St Laurent to Pierre Trudeau have helped the Commonwealth to survive its differences and evolve new patterns of practical co-operation. Under UN auspices, and with different degrees of success, Canadian troops have tried to keep the peace in Cyprus, the Middle East, the Congo and Kashmir. With less fanfare, Canadians have provided valuable expertise to a host of UN committees and other international organizations.

The myths are also bolstered by some painful negative evidence. When Diefenbaker loudly defied Washington he did little more than arouse American wrath. When his External Affairs Minister, Howard Green, lectured the great powers on the need for nuclear disarmament, he was soon revealed as a windy moralizer with little knowledge of his subject. Whatever the limitations of Liberal diplomacy, it cannot be said that the modern Conservative party has practised a workable alternative.

Yet the strategies of Quiet Diplomacy and Helpful Fixing *do* have limitations. Elegant in style and sometimes filled with moral fervour, our diplomacy has often failed the ultimate test for any foreign policy through being timid and short-sighted in the expression of national aspirations and the defence of national interests. These limitations are serious — and potentially fatal — at a time when the growing desire of Canadians to be free of American domination within our borders has become linked to a serious quest for a similar independence in our foreign policies.

There is one important case history which illustrates the drawbacks to our traditional diplomacy and about which most of the important facts are now established. Canada's twenty-year record of Quiet Diplomacy and Helpful Fixing in Vietnam is a sorry tale of good intentions and limited achievements undermined by bungling and political misjudgment and leaving a legacy of futility and guilt. For all its special features — and partly *because* of them — it casts serious doubt on the aims and methods of our diplomacy, especially in its dealings with Washington. Although this book is based on our experience in Vietnam, now fortunately ended, it is really about our differences with the United States, which continue and may well worsen.

* * * * *

Canada became involved in Vietnam in 1954 when it joined Poland and India on the International Control Commission, established by the Geneva Conference in the wake of the French defeat at Dien Bien Phu. The Commission was meant to supervise the disengagement of military forces, the exchange of prisoners and refugees and the peace between North and South Vietnam. After some initial success, the ICC soon became deadlocked and virtually impotent as hostilities resumed in the South and both the United States and North Vietnam began to intervene massively on the side of their allies. This is the subject of Chapter One.

Chapters Two and Three deal with the period 1964-1968 which saw the buildup of the American expeditionary force in South Vietnam, American bombing of North Vietnam, a succession of coups in Saigon and a variety of attempts to find a diplomatic solution to the military impasse. Several of these attempts involved Canadians, most notably the missions to Hanoi of Blair Seaborn and Chester Ronning.

Chapter Four takes up the story in 1972, with the belligerents approaching agreement on a ceasefire in their Paris talks and Canada under pressure to join Poland, Hungary and Indonesia on a new supervisory commission. This time Canada's role lasted only six months as the ICCS* soon reached deadlock and fighting continued across South Vietnam. When Ottawa finally announced that enough was enough and the Canadian contingent left Saigon on July 31, 1973, it ended nearly twenty years of erstwhile peacekeeping and peacemaking: two decades of frustration and failure.

Chapter Five sets this Vietnam experience in the larger context of Canadian foreign policy and especially relations with the United States. Despite Ottawa's brave words about our Vietnam role, Canada was neither impartial nor objective. Whatever our initial intentions, we soon became little more than American surrogates on both the ICC and the ICCS, carefully tending the interests of Washington and Saigon as well as dabbling in dubious intelligence work and selling the Americans part of the arms and ammunition with which they wrought such unparalleled destruction. Throughout the whole period Canadian leaders largely accepted Washington's view of a conflict which most of the world (including many Canadians) came increasingly to regard as a wicked and tragic misuse of American power. Faithful to the tenets of Quiet Diplomacy, Ottawa rarely tried with any real conviction to dissuade the Americans from their war aims or even to dissociate us from them, while allowing its own diplomatic initiatives to serve the American strategy of military

---

* I have followed common usage in referring to the supervisory commission established by the 1954 Geneva Conference as the International Control Commission (ICC) and to its successor as the International Commission of Control and Supervision (ICCS).

escalation. At every stage Ottawa's policies made Canada an accomplice of the Americans in their senseless and horrendous war.

It is not a happy story. But it is important to establish what went wrong and with the benefit of hindsight it is possible to suggest other courses of action that would have been more consistent with Canadian self-interest. At the very least we should no longer have any illusions — not only about the perils of peacekeeping and peacemaking, but also about the chances of influencing our powerful neighbour through Quiet Diplomacy. To study our Vietnam experience is to understand the ruthless use of power which is instinctive to any American Administration. It is a lesson that must be applied during all future confrontations, especially those that involve vital Canadian interests.

Yet we must not allow ourselves to lapse into what Robert Fulford has aptly called Diversionary Anti-Americanism — "diversionary not only because it keeps us from thinking about our own mistakes but also because it keeps away from our minds the guilt-feelings that lurk in many of us."[2] It might be tempting to make the Americans into the villains of the piece. It might even be comforting if we could believe that Ottawa always knew that the Americans were wrong about Vietnam and that Canadian support was given reluctantly, in response to overwhelming American pressure and through fear of American economic retaliation.

But this was never the case. Although the American pressures were often intense, they were always secondary since Canadian support was offered freely and out of genuine conviction. If the Americans did a snow job on the Canadian leaders, the Canadian leaders did an even bigger snow job on the Canadian people. More crucially, they fooled *themselves*, through a tragic misunderstanding of the issues in Southeast Asia and a misguided faith in the prowess of their own diplomacy. To the very end, Canada was an active and willing accomplice.

* * * * *

A personal note. I have covered and studied the Vietnam war since I went to Asia as a *Globe and Mail* correspondent in 1962. I wish I could claim that I was always a stern opponent of the American war and an outspoken critic of Canadian policies. *Mea culpa.* For some time I was a relative hawk over Vietnam and a staunch admirer of Canadian diplomacy, as well as a close friend of many of its most able and articulate practitioners. I hope the friendships have survived, but the views have certainly changed.

There was no sudden conversion; during a decade of reporting from Asia, Africa, the Middle East and Europe, I came to regard the Vietnam war and Canadian foreign policy with increasing scepticism. I have not lapsed into a sterile anti-Americanism, nor do I now regard the Vietnamese Communists as noble humanitarians and Canadian political leaders as unmitigated scoundrels. But mistakes were made − bad mistakes − and it seems important to nail them down. While I don't have all the answers, I hope this book poses the right questions, provides the raw material for others to use in reaching their own conclusions and − by analysing the failure of Canadian diplomacy over Vietnam − suggests ways to avoid similar mistakes in the future.

* * * * *

Many people have helped in the preparation of this book and were generous with their time and advice. Some would strongly dissent from my opinions and conclusions, for which I am solely responsible. I am grateful to a large number of Canadian and other officials who have furnished me with information, arguments and insights and whose desire for anonymity must be respected. Others can be named with an equal gratitude. They include — in alphabetical order — Fred Branfman, McGeorge Bundy, William Bundy, Gordon Fairweather, MP, Graeme Gibson, Walter Gordon, Ivan Head, John Holmes, Alex. I. Inglis, Don Luce, Senator Paul Martin, Kim Richard Nossal, G. A. H. Pearson, Nancy and John Pocock, Gary Porter, Chester Ronning, Doug Rowland, MP, Mitchell Sharp, MP, and Seymour Topping.

I would also like to thank Arthur Andrew, formerly Director-General of the Bureau of Asian and Pacific Affairs of the Department of External Affairs, for responding to my requests for factual information. Mrs Ruth Margaret Thompson of External Affairs and David Rhydwen of *The Globe and Mail* kindly allowed me to use their libraries.

Finally I would like to thank the editors of *The Globe and Mail* for more than a decade of support and encouragement, and Shirley Gibson and James Polk of The House of Anansi for their important contributions to this book.

one

We have always been ready to be a
"mediator", even at risk of
becoming a busybody.

Lester B. Pearson

It was summer in Geneva. For more than three months the sparkling capital had been home to a motley collection of diplomats — among them Americans, British, French and Russians, as well as a confusing assortment of Asians, including Chinese, Koreans, Vietnamese, Laotians and Cambodians of various political persuasions and tangled historical rivalries. Some were hardened veterans of the conference circuit, men whose names evoked the memory of many an earlier crisis, men like John Foster Dulles, Anthony Eden, Georges Bidault and Vyacheslav Molotov. Others — like Chou En-lai and Pham Van Dong — were less familiar figures in the elegant halls of the Palais des Nations, but they spoke with confidence and force for a continent whose revolutionary aspirations were already challenging the interests of the established powers.

It was July 21, 1954. Champagne corks were popping in the Delegates Lounge. Peace was in the air and the diplomats had cause to celebrate. There had been an armistice in Korea for nearly a year, but in Vietnam the plight of the encircled French forces at Dien Bien Phu had raised the possibility of American military intervention and even the use of nuclear weapons. Now — after weeks of fierce debate and intricate bargaining — the Geneva Agreements had established another ceasefire, this time among France, its Vietnamese allies and the Viet Minh forces of Ho Chi Minh. While each of the Great

3

Powers had serious reservations about the terms of the truce, each was anxious to end a conflict which had dragged on for nearly eight years and which carried the threat of another major confrontation between the Communist and Western worlds. Although the Agreements were slapdash and imprecise, at least they held out some promise of detente in Southeast Asia. For the moment everyone could breathe a little easier.

On that balmy summer day it would have taken a determined Cassandra to predict that there would still be fighting in Indochina after another 20 years, that a vast American expeditionary force would have come and gone — leaving horrendous carnage and destruction in its wake — and that Vietnam would become as divisive an issue in the Western world as Spain had been for an earlier generation, rending the very fabric of American society and straining the loyalties of America's allies. When Canadians read in their newspapers that their diplomats and soldiers would soon be helping to supervise the truce in Indochina, they, too, had little reason to suspect that their country would be entangled with Vietnam for nearly two decades of frustrated peacekeeping and ineffective diplomacy and that their nation's reputation would be tarnished by the support which Ottawa would give to the American war.

From the start Ottawa had doubts about becoming involved in Indochina. In late July government spokesmen let it be known that Canada was joining the International Control Commission in Vietnam (and similar commissions in Laos and Cambodia) with great reluctance. External Affairs Minister Pearson warned in a statement: "We have no illusions that the task we are undertaking will be either easy or of short duration." In a personal message to British Foreign Secretary Anthony Eden, Pearson said that Canada had no disposition to evade the new responsibility "which may, however, turn out to be as onerous as it certainly was unsought."[1]

Not for the last time, Canada was nominated for a peace-keeping role by a conference in which it had not taken part and under a mandate which it had done little to shape. Not for the last time, either, the pressures were intense. The Cold War was still a frightening reality and there were few Canadians who questioned the concept of a monolithic Communist bloc intent on aggression and subversion to achieve world domination. It seemed that a wider war had been narrowly averted in Korea and that only a sustained effort at Geneva had prevented a similar confrontation in Indochina. For all its doubts about the Geneva Agreements, Ottawa was quick to acknowledge that a Canadian refusal to participate would be highly irresponsible, since it could easily jeopardize the fragile peace.

Ottawa really had no choice. With strong support from Prime Minister Louis St Laurent, Pearson had committed Canada to playing a full part in the international organization of peace and security. As a young diplomat in Geneva, he had watched with anguish and despair as the League of Nations failed in 1935 to halt Italian aggression in Ethiopia. In Pearson's view this failure was a direct cause of World War Two and his own government was one of the culprits. It was a searing experience and it helped to form one of his most basic beliefs: ". . . that only by collective international action and by a consequent limitation of national sovereignty through the acceptance of international commitments, can peace and security be established and maintained, and human survival ensured."[2]

As World War Two came to an end, Pearson and his Canadian colleagues played an important role in establishing the United Nations. When the UN proved powerless to prevent the growth of Cold War tensions, Canada helped to form the North Atlantic Treaty Organization which Ottawa regarded as a defensive response to Stalin's moves in eastern and central Europe. After North Korean forces crossed the 38th parallel, Canada joined the majority of UN members in condemning the invasion. By sending troops to fight under the UN command, Ottawa was backing its belief that wider wars could only be averted if the nations accepted their collective obligations, however costly these might prove. Yet the Canadian contributions were never made as part of a crusade against Communism which aimed at total victory. Since the devil was strong, you had to bargain with him — in Vietnam, as in Korea, Ottawa had long favoured a negotiated truce.

With this background Canada could hardly have refused a call to supervise the peace in Indochina. Yet it had to pay the price — again, not for the last time — of being named to a peacekeeping body before it had given its formal consent and before it even knew the terms of its mandate. The Geneva

6

powers were in such a hurry to conclude their conference (largely to meet a deadline imposed upon them by French Prime Minister Pierre Mendès-France), that by the time their invitation reached Ottawa, the Agreements were already in effect and there were only three weeks before the full implementation of the ceasefire. It seemed largely a formality, not to mention face-saving, when Ottawa took a week to study the Agreements before announcing its acceptance.

It is hardly surprising that Canada was chosen. Although Suez still lay in the future, Canadians at the UN had already shown a major interest in peacekeeping. A Western nation was needed to balance a Communist member and a non-aligned country on the troika of the ICC; Canada was one of the few Western nations with no history as a colonial power and it could also provide French-speaking diplomats and soldiers. Canadians had been active in Korea, both as combatants and negotiators; in the latter role they had demonstrated a certain independence of Washington which had been noted by the Communist powers and such non-aligned nations as India. Even then, however, there was some doubt about the extent of Canadian independence. Chinese Prime Minister Chou En-lai had already complained (to the Indian ambassador in Peking) that Canada had succumbed to American pressure in voting for the UN resolution condemning China for aggression in Korea — a charge which Pearson later described as accurate.[3]

But it was deemed more important for the Western member to be independent of France rather than the United States (Belgium had been considered and rejected on these grounds). In the end Canada was proposed by Chou, reportedly on the urging of Indian Foreign Minister Krishna Menon. In view of later developments it is important to note that Canada was not proposed by the United States whose chief delegate, Gen. Walter Bedell Smith, told Washington that he preferred Belgium.[4] There was certainly no American pres-

7

sure to have Canada join the Commission. Disgruntled by the proceedings at Geneva, and fearful of Chinese and North Vietnamese expansion, the Americans had dissociated themselves from the Agreements (while promising not to use force, or the threat of force, to overthrow them). There was even concern in Ottawa that membership on the ICC would only make relations with Washington more difficult.[5]

That was one reason for the doubts. Another was the lack of any role in the settlement for the United Nations: a role which would have been much more in line with Pearsonian diplomacy. Ironically, there were no strenuous Canadian objections to the *composition* of the Commission, with Canada as the Western nation, Poland as the Communist representative and India as the neutral chairman. This troika arrangement was deemed preferable to the situation in Korea where each side was meant to nominate two "neutral" members to the supervisory commission. While the UN side named two genuine neutrals in Sweden and Switzerland, the Communists put forward Poland and Czechoslovakia, who were anything but impartial.*

But Ottawa was openly apprehensive about the *terms* under which the ICC would operate. Its first task was to supervise the regrouping of French Union and Viet Minh forces and the transfer of territory, as well as the exchange of prisoners-of-war and the flow of refugees between the two new political entities of North and South Vietnam. Operating from team sites on both sides of the 17th parallel, the ICC was also to supervise the military provisions of the Agreements, including the prohibition against either side establishing new military bases or permitting foreign powers to

---

* The Communists defined a neutral nation as one which had not taken part in the war. Nineteen years later, with the ICC moribund, Canada vowed it would never participate in another unworkable troika, while accepting membership on another two-on-two commission.

8

establish bases, increasing its armaments or the number of foreign military personnel. Beyond the 14 fixed team sites, the Demilitarized Zone astride the 17th parallel and "zones of action" along land and sea frontiers, the movement of ICC mobile teams was subject to the agreement of the Vietnamese authorities, either Northern or Southern.

The ICC was given authority to investigate and mediate as well as to observe: theoretically it could tell both parties what measures they should take to settle their disputes, but it had no powers of enforcement. On routine matters the Commission could make its recommendations by majority vote, but its decisions had to be unanimous on the key questions of violations, or threats of violations, which might lead to a resumption of hostilities. Even then, majority and minority reports could be sent to the Geneva powers. Finally, the ICC was to supervise free general elections throughout Vietnam in July 1956, with the implication that the Commission would be through its work in two years.

It took no great political genius to predict that a mandate so full of loopholes and so short of specific powers might prove impossible to enforce, especially since the governments in both Hanoi and Saigon were quick to show their dissatisfaction with the Geneva settlement.* Once committed to the task, however, Ottawa maintained a brave show of optimism — at least in the early stages. The Canadians were on the job

---

* The only documents *signed* at Geneva were ceasefire agreements between the High Command of the French Union Forces and the Commander-in-Chief of the People's Army of Vietnam. The Final Declaration of the conference was neither a treaty nor an agreement. It summed up the ceasefire arrangements, contained various unilateral statements and promised little more than to give international blessing to the independence of Laos and Cambodia and to establish two political entities in Vietnam. It was not signed by any of the delegations and it was opposed by the two most directly concerned: the Communist and non-Communist Vietnamese representatives.

in August; in December, Pearson told the House of Commons that the ICC was working well. Nor was this mere bravado: despite logistical difficulties and complex disputes between the two sides, about 190,000 French Union troops and 80,000 Viet Minh were being regrouped under ICC supervision. This regrouping and the transfer of territories on either side of the 17th parallel were completed by May 18, 1955 — as stipulated at Geneva. During these first 300 days the ICC performed a remarkable task in supervising the separation of the former belligerents without any serious incident. It was an achievement in which the Canadian diplomats and soldiers rightly took enormous pride.

Even during this period, however, there was evidence that Hanoi was determined to restrict the Commission's activities and that the Poles and the Canadians were finding it increasingly difficult to work together. By January 1955, External Affairs officials were complaining that the Commission's effectiveness was starting to deteriorate. Although the ICC supervised the exchange of 65,000 prisoners of the French for 11,000 captured by the Viet Minh, each side claimed that the other was holding on to thousands more. There was a similar dispute over civilian internees which was never fully resolved and which was to flare up again after the Paris Agreement of 1973.

Refugees came to pose an even greater problem. About 850,000 eventually went to the South, mainly Roman Catholics from centres in the North where the French still had temporary control, while only a few thousand moved from South to North. Canadians on the ICC complained that the North Vietnamese were denying exit permits to tens of thousands of other would-be refugees, that local authorities were frustrating their investigations and that ICC intervention on behalf of any individual was often tantamount to a sentence of death. For the first time the ICC found itself unable to act unanimously, with Canada drawing attention to the

10

refugee problem in an appendage to the Commission's third interim report.

In March and again in May, Pearson rose in the House of Commons to make the first public criticisms of the ICC's work by one of its members. Without divulging any details, he accused the Communist side of hampering the ICC and maintained that "terrible things" were being done (a clear reference to the plight of the would-be refugees). Whatever the provocation, this set the pattern for hundreds of Canadian statements in the years ahead. While Ottawa would also criticise the South Vietnamese and the Americans for violating the Geneva Agreements, its strongest language was always reserved for the Communists. Already — and perhaps inevitably — the Commission was starting to divide on Cold War lines.

If May was a watershed for the ICC, it was even more of a milestone for Washington and Saigon. In February the Americans had taken over from the French in training the South Vietnamese armed forces. In May they took a more fateful step in announcing their unequivocal support for Ngo Dinh Diem, the new strongman who had just ended months of turmoil in Saigon by routing his enemies among the powerful sects and outflanking Emperor Bao Dai, the favourite of the French. With American backing Diem moved quickly to consolidate his control: in July he declared that the elections to unify the country which the Geneva Agreements had scheduled for July 1956, would not be held in the South. He was supported by American spokesmen who noted that neither Saigon nor Washington had signed the Agreements and that it would be impossible to hold genuinely free elections in the North.

This decision not only deprived the ICC of one of its stipulated duties, it also drew the battle lines for the conflict that lay ahead and dashed any remaining hopes that the Commission's work might be completed at the end of the original

11

two years. From this point the ICC began its steady decline towards futility and impotence. Its major remaining task was to supervise those provisions of the Agreements which were meant to prevent a military buildup by either side and any renewal of hostilities. Even if the Commission members had always been able to agree among themselves, their job would still have proved impossible, since it soon became evident that Hanoi and Saigon were moving toward a confrontation and were unlikely to be deterred by terms imposed upon them in a far-off European city and supervised by a few hundred foreign diplomats and soldiers whose work could easily be disrupted and whose advice and criticisms could painlessly be ignored.

In the North, Ho and his colleagues felt that the Geneva Conference had robbed them of the fruits of their great victory over the French. Only pressure from the Russians and the Chinese had compelled them to accept the 17th parallel as a temporary limit to their ambitions for a united Vietnam under their control; when the Viet Minh regrouped above the parallel, they left behind thousands of cadres, most of them southerners who remained in their native villages to preserve their political base.

In Saigon, Diem was confident of American support in denying the Communists and their supporters any place in South Vietnam's political life. In the aftermath of the Korean War and the McCarthy era, with the militantly anti-Communist John Foster Dulles as Secretary of State, Washington was expounding the so-called domino theory which maintained that all of Southeast Asia would be lost to Communist expansion unless the line was drawn in Vietnam. Following the Geneva Conference, Dulles had set up the Southeast Asia Treaty Organization, which formally took it upon itself to defend South Vietnam, Laos and Cambodia from outside aggression.

From the start American efforts were more than merely defensive. Even before the rise of Diem, sabotage teams

12

under the legendary Col. Edward G. Lansdale of the Central Intelligence Agency had been operating in North Vietnam in direct violation of Washington's promise to refrain from using force against the Geneva settlement;[6] it was also Lansdale who helped to mastermind Diem's rise to power. After Diem repudiated the Geneva provision for national elections there was a slow but steady growth of violence in the South. Historians differ over whether this violence was started by the Viet Minh cadres who had remained below the 17th parallel, or by Diem himself.[7] The point is somewhat academic, since, by refusing a legitimate political role to the nationalists who had spearheaded the great victory over the French, Diem made it inevitable that they would eventually renew their insurgency. Between 1957 and 1959, incidents of violence were increasingly reported throughout the countryside and attributed by Saigon to the Viet Minh. At the same time Diem launched a savage campaign which largely destroyed the Viet Minh infrastructure in the villages, forcing its surviving members to flee to the slums of Saigon or regroup in the jungles and swamps which had been their bases against the French. When the southerners appealed to North Vietnam for assistance, Hanoi was reportedly at first reluctant to send material help, judging that the time was not yet ripe for a major uprising.[8]

From early 1959 the southern Communists (and some non-Communist supporters) increasingly resorted to terrorism and sabotage in reply to Diem's repression. In July, two US military advisers were killed in a raid at Bien Hoa airbase near Saigon: the first American casualties of the conflict. In response the United States increased the flow of advisers and military supplies to South Vietnam. By autumn the insurgents were fielding units of battalion size against regular army formations. Diplomatic charges and counter-charges escalated with the fighting: in April 1960, Hanoi accused Washington of turning South Vietnam into "a US military base for

13

the preparation of a new war." Saigon responded in November with an accusation that North Vietnam had launched aggression against the South by infiltrating troops through Laos. In December, the southern guerrillas formed a political body, the National Liberation Front, which included non-Communists elements.* By then the war was truly launched.

* * * * *

Now that both sides were committed to the conflict, the ICC faced an impossible task. With its long coastline and land frontiers with Cambodia and Laos, as well as along the Demilitarized Zone, South Vietnam had innumerable entry points for military reinforcements and supplies; it also had an increasing number of airfields. Even with full co-operation from the Vietnamese authorities, the Commission's fixed and mobile teams could hardly have covered all these adequately. Co-operation, of course, was a benefit that the ICC seldom enjoyed. As early as 1954, Hanoi frustrated ICC attempts to inspect its routes to China; later it was Saigon's turn to be obstreperous. Diem's regime gave only the most grudging assistance to the Commission after France dissolved its High Command in April 1956. From late 1961, Saigon consistently refused to let the ICC make a multitude of proposed inspections, while admitting that it had requested more US advisers and weapons to counter "aggression" directed by Hanoi. Even when inspections were permitted, they were often rendered farcical through Vietnamese obstruction. For example, the Commission depended on the Vietnamese for transport: this was usually non-existent or hopelessly

---

* The National Liberation Front (NLF) and the People's Liberation Army (PLA) are formal titles for the Communist-dominated resistance movement and its fighting arm in South Vietnam. I use them in preference to "Viet Cong" which has derogatory connotations.

14

inadequate. It is a measure of the Commission's plight that it failed to inspect a *single* military base in either North or South Vietnam.

To make matters much worse, the ICC was almost always at loggerheads: an inevitable result of having Western and Communist members under a neutral chairman. With some flair — and a great deal of stubbornness — the Poles protected the interests of Hanoi and the NLF: a perfectly natural Communist response. At first most of the Canadians hoped that the Commission could operate impartially — in other words, effectively. But they soon found themselves — diplomats and soldiers alike — taking the side of Saigon and Washington. Even in the early months of the Commission's work, the Canadians were reporting to Ottawa that they were being forced — because of strong Polish support for Hanoi — to act in a way that made them appear to be apologists for Saigon and the French Union High Command.

The Canadians sought to justify their partiality by drawing a distinction between their roles as "advocates" and "judges". Clearly they were *advocates* of a Western point of view — why else had they been named to the job? But in *judging* any particular issue — such as an alleged violation of the Agreements — they would try to be objective.[9] In practice this distinction soon proved to be little more than sophistry. On occasion Canada *did* criticise Saigon or Washington; increasingly it was zealous and messianic in trying to pin down Communist violations. Eventually the Canadians became almost mirror-images of the Poles, even to the point of turning a blind eye on US arms shipments and other violations of the Agreements.

Although Ottawa always denied that its men were guilty of such blatant partiality, there is evidence that they were, and that the government did nothing to stop it. Hugh Campbell, a retired RCAF squadron leader who served on the ICC from 1961 to 1963, later said that he was "bloody ashamed

15

of some of the things I was required to do because of the External Affairs Department's policy in Vietnam." Members of the Canadian delegation regularly ignored breaches of the Agreements, he added, "like pretending I didn't see a flight of US helicopters overhead . . . or American warships in the harbour." According to Campbell, there was nothing on paper telling the Canadian officers to cover for the Americans, but they knew their careers would have suffered if they hadn't.[10]

The Canadians drew a further distinction between serving the interests of the United States and those of South Vietnam. Sensitive to charges that they were merely American stooges, they maintained that they were often acting to ensure that the views of *Saigon* received a fair hearing on the Commission, which might otherwise neglect the interests of millions of non-Communist South Vietnamese. But this seems even greater sophistry, since none of the successive Saigon regimes ever retained wide popularity among the people it fitfully controlled and since none could long remain in power without American support.

Canadian partiality was a psychological, as well as a political, response: the result of thrusting Canadian foreign service officers − most of them young and new to Asia − into the maelstrom of a divided nation whose history and traditions were far removed from Western patterns. If all the Vietnamese were strange at first, the Southerners at least seemed more approachable and human. Despite its traces of French colonial elegance, Hanoi was a grim, austere and typically Communist capital; Saigon may have been seething with corruption but it had vitality and a veneer of Western influence. Although the South Vietnamese officials were often difficult and obstructive, the Canadians found them much easier to get on with than their Communist counterparts. It was also natural for the Canadians to mix with their American colleagues in Saigon, as they would in any other capital. If this was natural, it was also unfortunate. During their time in Vietnam, many of the brightest Canadian diplomats became converts to the most hawkish American views, even to the point of ignoring all the mounting evidence that American political and military assessments were either deliberately distorted or else based on little more than wishful thinking.

Often, however, it was more a case of previous conviction than on-the-spot conversion. Some of the Canadians came to Vietnam from postings in Eastern Europe; they never seemed to grasp the crucial distinction that the Vietnamese Communists were not puppets imposed by an outside power but veteran revolutionaries who had seized the leadership of a genuine war of national liberation. It was a fatal drawback that in the late 1950s and early 1960s, External Affairs had no senior diplomats with long experience of Southeast Asia who could have interpreted the turmoil in terms of Indochinese history, rather than the sterile patterns of Cold War demonology, who could have seen that the Americans were doomed to repeat the mistakes of the French and who might have persuaded Ottawa to modify its support for Saigon and Washington.

The Canadian delegation always seemed to lack such broader perspectives. In the early years most of the Canadians were deeply shocked and permanently affected by Hanoi's blatant disregard of the Geneva accords and its brutal treatment of aspiring refugees. Scorning accusations that they had been ideologically seduced by the Americans, these Canadians would proudly assert that they had developed their hardline views on the basis of their own experience of the North Vietnamese in the late 1950s — before the Americans were deeply involved. This early obsession with the sins of the North Vietnamese and their Southern supporters would make it relatively easy for the Canadians to gloss over the shortcomings and weaknesses of successive Saigon regimes.

17

Another crucial factor was the sheer professional pride with which the Canadians approached their peacekeeping assignment. They always had an abiding faith in their ability to do the job better than anyone else. This made them obsessed with the letter — rather than the spirit — of the Geneva accords: an obsession which was strengthened every time the Poles blocked commission investigations of alleged Communist truce violations. It was a fixation on the means rather than the ends, on the machinery of policy rather than the policy itself. Determined to prove that the Geneva settlement could be made to work in spite of Communist obstruction, the Canadians rarely took the time to question what the fighting was all about.

The Canadian military delegates were also inclined to adopt rigid and inflexible views. Many came to fraternise and sympathise with the American advisers and, later, with officers of the vast American expeditionary force. According to charges by Canadian journalists, some Canadian officers functioned as spies, passing on first-hand observations of North Vietnam, including assessments of the US bombing. Pearson and Paul Martin, who succeeded him as External Affairs Minister, strongly denied these charges. But the charges were later confirmed by another retired officer, Brigadier Donald Ketcheson, who said that during his service on the ICC in 1958 and 1959, he regularly furnished the Central Intelligence Agency with information about Communist troop movements. External Affairs was unoffically aware of this, and "looked the other way".[11] Further confirmation came from Dr David G. Marr, a former Marine intelligence captain. Dr Marr claimed that while serving in Hawaii in early 1964, he handled a CIA report which indicated that information about anti-aircraft installations in Hanoi had been received from a Canadian member of the ICC.[12]

Perhaps there is no cause for indignation, or even surprise. As we shall see, Canadian leaders were making strong statements throughout this period which accepted Washington's view of the conflict and condemned North Vietnamese aggression in the South. Many Canadians on the spot probably thought they would be derelict in their duty if they didn't help defeat this aggression: to the military members, it may have seemed a logical extension of their peacekeeping role. But the evidence of Canadian spying is another sad commentary on Ottawa's pretension that Canada acted independently on the ICC and was never a mere surrogate for the United States.

If the Canadians found it only natural to side with the Americans and the South Vietnamese, they were also pushed to extremes in this direction by the attitude of the Indians on the ICC. As a leading exponent of non-alignment, India was anxious to strike a long-term balance in the Commission's work and opposed attempts by either the Canadians or the Poles to make short-run propaganda gains. "This made the Indians formidable but difficult partners", according to the diplomatic assessment of a senior External Affairs official.[13] In fact it kept the Canadians in a state of almost constant apoplexy. To visit Saigon at any time during the 1960s was to hear impassioned Canadian tirades against the Indians for their obstructiveness, hypocrisy and sheer bloody-mindedness.

While the Indians sometimes sided with the Canadians against the Poles, most Canadians on the ICC remained convinced that they were leaning over backwards to avoid offending the Communist side. True or not, this feeling had an unfortunate result. It effectively demolished a major prop of Pearson's foreign policy: the Ottawa-New Delhi axis which had been fostered through the early 1950s and which Ottawa viewed as an important bridge between the affluent West and the Third World, a source of unity in the Commonwealth and a force for peace and sanity in a troubled international community. By the time the ICC finally sank into oblivion, so many Canadian and Indian foreign service officers had

19

struggled and squabbled with each other for so long that the Ottawa-New Delhi axis was a dead letter in diplomacy. This was a sad loss; it also revealed a major inconsistency in Canadian foreign policy. Ottawa always argued that it had influence in places like New Delhi because it was a loyal ally of the United States *and* capable of independent action. As the Indians certainly saw it, the Canadian performance in Vietnam revealed the frequent hollowness of this pretension.

On one important occasion, however, the Canadians and the Indians did manage to agree. From 1960 the Commission had received frequent complaints from Saigon that the sabotage and terrorism in the South were directed from Hanoi. Over Polish objections, the ICC instructed its legal committee to investigate the charges. The result — in July 1962 — was a special report to Britain and the Soviet Union (co-chairmen of the Geneva Conference) which was signed by Canada and India and from which Poland dissented. This majority report said that North Vietnam was breaking the Geneva Agreements by seeking to overthrow the Saigon government through subversion and interference, including the dispatch of "armed and unarmed personnel, arms, and munitions and other supplies." On the other hand, the report noted the increasing American military aid to Saigon, as well as the growing number of American advisers, and accused South Vietnam of also breaking the Agreement by forming a "factual military alliance" with the United States.

This became the most famous and frequently cited ICC report. In the years ahead Canadian spokesmen would use it to support their contention that Canada was always ready to criticise either or both sides to the conflict, depending on the evidence. At the same time the Americans would use *part* of the report to support *their* contention that South Vietnam was the victim of aggression from the North.

The reality was much more complex, since the uprising in the South was at least partly provoked by Diem's refusal to hold elections and his crackdown on the Viet Minh cadres. Despite Hanoi's initial reluctance to become involved, there is no doubt, however, that in the early 1960s the North Vietnamese were sending military supplies down the Ho Chi Minh Trail through Laos and Cambodia. Seeking to establish control over the NLF, they were also infiltrating men, although in the early years these were mainly southerners who had regrouped to the North in 1954 and were returning to their own areas. Most historians now agree that there was nothing like an invasion from the North until *after* the United States had openly sent troops to fight with the South Vietnamese.[14] Until the massive American intervention, Saigon's forces were succumbing to southern guerrillas who relied more on the local population and on materials captured from the South Vietnamese army than they did on assistance from North Vietnam. According to the Pentagon Papers*, American intelligence reports were stating as late as 1964 that "the primary sources of Communist strength in South Vietnam are indigenous", arising out of the revolutionary social aims of the Communists and their identification with the independence struggle against the French.[15] In this sense the ICC report helped to perpetrate one of the most misguided myths about the conflict despite its attempt at impartiality.

Another part of the 1962 report was less noted but equally significant. This described "a near-complete breakdown" in the Commission's activities, complaining that its teams had been "persistently denied the right to control and inspect" in

---

* The Pentagon Papers are a study of the whole US involvement in Vietnam from 1945 to 1967 which was prepared under stringent secrecy within the Defense Department on the orders of former Defense Secretary Robert McNamara. Portions of the Papers were made available to the *New York Times* and other newspapers in 1971 by Daniel Ellsberg, a former Rand Corporation employee who had worked as a government consultant.

South Vietnam since December 1961, that its observers were regarded as spies by both Vietnamese governments and that the ICC had no power to enforce its decisions. These were simple statements of fact. As fighting spread throughout the South in 1963 and 1964 the Commission was largely impotent and almost moribund. Acknowledging this situation in September 1964, External Affairs Minister Paul Martin told the House of Commons that while Canada was not withdrawing from the ICC, it "was not anxious to cling to this particular assignment."

In fact, senior officials had made regular assessments of Canada's position in the years since 1954. The need to maintain a Canadian contingent on all three Indochina commissions of up to 135 military personnel and 35 civilians was a considerable strain on the Departments of National Defence and External Affairs; it was also costing the Canadian taxpayer an average of about $1-million a year. As early as April 1956, External's Under-Secretary, Jules Leger, had told MPs that the Department would like to see the work of the Commissions wound up as speedily as possible.

But political arguments always outweighed considerations of manpower and expense. On several occasions officials drew up balance sheets which listed the arguments in favour of staying on or getting out. Each time the decision was taken to remain. Officials maintained that there was no great pressure on Ottawa from the United States; indeed, as the Americans became increasingly involved in a major war, they were impatient with the Commission's work and often made their impatience abundantly clear.[16] Even so, Ottawa was showing a growing sensitivity to charges that the Canadians on the ICC were little more than American agents: it was frequently argued that if Canada did withdraw, this would be widely seen — at home and abroad — as an American directive. This was probably an accurate assessment; it also indicated the extent to which Canadian foreign

22

policy was already considered to be subservient to American demands.

There was one main reason for staying on the ICC. Time and time again in Ottawa, the arguments for withdrawal were outweighed by the contention that sometime, somehow, somewhere, there would have to be negotiations to end the war. These negotiations would be arranged through diplomatic channels: Canada's access to Hanoi as an ICC member could be important in establishing the first contacts between the Americans and the North Vietnamese. Even more important, the negotiations would almost certainly be based on "a return to the Geneva Agreements" — a pious phrase which all the parties used from time to time. So there was a real need to preserve some vestige of the Agreements on the ground in Vietnam, both as a framework on which the negotiations might be started and as an international presence which could be reactivated to supervise a new ceasefire. Since a Canadian withdrawal could cause the ICC to disappear completely, it would be a highly irresponsible act.

Subsequent events showed that all these arguments were wrong. As we shall see, the "Canadian channel" to Hanoi was used by the Americans mainly to deliver ultimatums; when Ottawa used it for an independent initiative, Washington reacted with dismay. President Lyndon Johnson and Secretary of State Dean Rusk often boasted that there was no shortage of places in which they could contact the North Vietnamese; in fact, the ICC played no part in arranging the eventual negotiations in Paris. These negotiations were based on the existing military and political situation, rather than upon Agreements which dated back to 1954 and which had long proved unworkable and unrealistic. The ICC was not involved in the ceasefire which followed the Paris Agreement of 1973; instead a new commission was established which implicitly disavowed the troika principle. Finally, if the experience with the ICCS is any guide, a Canadian withdrawal would not have demolished the ICC. India and Poland would almost certainly have remained and another Western or Western-leaning nation might have been found to take over Canada's thankless task.

If Canada *had* decided to withdraw from the ICC in the early 1960s, the evidence presented in the 1962 majority report would have provided ample justification. The report not only criticised both sides for breaking the Geneva Agreements, it also described a virtual paralysis of the Commission itself: these were almost exactly the same grounds that Ottawa advanced for leaving the ICCS in 1973. By 1962 the Canadians had been in Vietnam for eight years, instead of the two years envisaged at Geneva. A Canadian withdrawal at that point would have been honourable and reasonable: we had tried hard and could not be unduly blamed for the Commission's failure.

A Canadian withdrawal would also have been consistent with some aspects of the foreign policy of the Diefenbaker government which had been in power since 1957. Diefenbaker not only distrusted the senior officials of the External Affairs Department (whom he called "Pearsonalities"), he was also philosophically and temperamentally opposed to the strategies of Quiet Diplomacy and Helpful Fixing. His External Affairs Minister, Howard Green, had similar attitudes. In February 1960, Green told the House of Commons that

> The time has come to drop the idea that Canada's role in world affairs is to be an honest broker between the nations. We must decide instead that our role is to determine the right stand to take on problems, keeping in mind the Canadian background and, above all, using Canadian common sense. In effect, the time has come to take an independent approach.

While the Conservatives' objectives were laudable, their performance was lamentable. With a simplistic and sloganeering approach to world problems, Diefenbaker and Green

24

lurched from disaster to disaster, losing the respect of other governments which had grown accustomed to the smoother faces of Pearson and his disciples. As Peter Newman has noted: "The notion Canadians so long cherished that their country counted as an influential power in world affairs did not survive the Diefenbaker Years."[17]

While Diefenbaker avidly pursued trade with Communist nations, he made a point of thundering against international Communism at the United Nations and on a multitude of other platforms. To the extent that he considered Vietnam, his anti-Communism outweighed his suspicions of Washington. As late as March 1965, when he was back in opposition, Diefenbaker spoke out in support of the domino theory, arguing that if the Americans evacuated Vietnam, all of Southeast Asia would ultimately fall to the Communists.

But Vietnam was never a matter of pressing concern for Diefenbaker and his cabinet. Aside from mounting domestic problems, they were more involved with such issues as trade with Cuba, nuclear warheads on Canadian soil, disarmament and Britain's approach to the European Economic Community. Nor was world attention yet focused on Vietnam: while the violence in the South was steadily increasing, both the Americans and the North Vietnamese were still playing relatively limited roles and the possibility of a wider conflict still seemed fairly remote. During this period Washington's support for the Diem regime received relatively little criticism among the Canadian public: it would be several years before the anti-war movement was in full cry.

Despite his apparent disdain for the role of honest broker, Green frequently proclaimed Canada's role as a world peacekeeper and delivered quaint homilies on Ottawa's diplomatic prowess. In March 1962, he told the House of Commons that the future of Indochina "will depend upon what Red China decides to do, possibly on what the United States decides to do, and possibly on what some other countries decide to do. However, we are able to exercise a good deal of influence on all these countries." To the extent that it was considered in Peking and Washington, this boast must have evoked both astonishment and mirth.

In the same simplistic survey, Green charged that the Communists had been at the root of most of the trouble in South Vietnam and that American actions were largely defensive. Reflecting the views of his senior officials, he added that it might take a long time to work out a settlement and that "I do not see any prospect of Canada being able to leave the Vietnam Commission at an early date."

At any rate, Canada missed a rare chance to disengage from Vietnam during the Diefenbaker years. In April 1963 the Liberals were returned to power as a minority government. Both Pearson and Martin were determined to repair the ravages that Diefenbaker and Green had bestowed on Canadian foreign policies: Quiet Diplomacy and Helpful Fixing were very much back in style. More crucially, Pearson and Martin largely accepted the American view of the Vietnam conflict as a clear-cut case of aggression by a Communist power against a "free world" ally that was defending Western interests and deserved Western support. While Canada — in Martin's words — was not anxious to cling to its assignment, it would have struck the Liberals as the height of folly to cause a crisis on the ICC.

* * * * *

In the first year of the new Liberal government the conflict in Vietnam began turning into full-scale war while the ICC looked on helplessly. As the PLA extended its control over large areas of the South Vietnam countryside, Saigon reeled from crisis to crisis. In January 1964, the military junta which had overthrown and executed Diem three months earlier was in turn overthrown by Gen. Nguyen Khanh.

26

Washington was quick to embrace the new leader, promising further economic and military aid and threatening to expand the war if the Communists persisted in their aggression. Fearing a complete collapse of the South Vietnamese forces, the US sent 5,000 more military advisers to Saigon in July, bringing the total of American servicemen in the country to 21,000.

The stage was being set for a major extension of the conflict. The United States had mounted clandestine seaborne attacks against North Vietnam from February 1964, while planning to obtain a Congressional resolution that the Administration regarded as the equivalent to a declaration of war.[18] In early August the Administration found its pretext when North Vietnamese PT boats attacked two US destroyers on intelligence patrol in the Gulf of Tonkin. This was followed by US reprisal raids — the first bombing of the North — while Congress passed the so-called Tonkin Gulf Resolution which gave President Johnson wide powers of military action in Southeast Asia. At the same time the Administration reached a "general consensus" that the air attacks against the North would have to be resumed on a sustained basis, most likely early in the new year.[19]

Again the Communists provided the Americans with a convenient pretext. In February 1965, the PLA launched a raid against Pleiku airbase, killing eight Americans. In retaliation Johnson again called out his aircraft: by early March, Operation Rolling Thunder was bringing bombing raids to the North on an almost daily basis.

With the start of the bombing Hanoi demanded the withdrawal of the five ICC teams in North Vietnam, stating that it could no longer guarantee their safety. In the House of Commons, Martin described this reason as insufficient, pointing out that only two of the five team sites were located in the general area of the US strikes. He added that the enforced withdrawal was

27

an obvious and very serious illustration of the way the work of the Commission has been hindered by North Vietnam. For years the Northern teams have not been allowed to conduct meaningful controls, but their presence was symbolic of the Geneva settlement and North Vietnam's acceptance of it.

It is reasonable to surmise that Hanoi was anxious to deprive the Canadians on the teams of any chance to observe (and report to the Americans) the results of the bombing or the extent of the increased military and economic aid that was coming from the Soviet Union and China. But the teams had long been hindered in their work: their ouster had little practical effect, except to indicate that the Commission was now totally powerless to stop the hostilities, or even to report on them accurately.

Yet the ICC made one last attempt to honour its mandate. In March 1965, the Commission concluded that the American bombings were a further violation of the Geneva Agreements. The Canadians felt that this gave a distorted picture of the situation and added a minority statement prepared by Blair Seaborn, the chief Canadian delegate. At least implicitly, the Canadian statement justified the bombings by describing them as a response to Communist attacks in the South:

> In the view of the Canadian Delegation, they do not stem from any essentially new factors in the situation in Vietnam, nor can they be seen in isolation; rather, they are dramatic manifestations of a continuing instability which has, as its most important cause, the deliberate and persistent pursuit of aggressive but largely covert policies by North Vietnam directed against South Vietnam.

While claiming to be even-handed in their judgments, the Canadians were again leaning over backwards to support the United States. There was a significant legal and political difference between the American bombing of North Vietnam — a clear-cut case of aggression by one state against another — and Hanoi's support for an initially indigenous uprising in the southern area of a country which the Geneva Agreements had explicitly recognised as *one* nation.

The Commission's 1965 report was its last important initiative. In March, Washington began its military buildup in the South, landing two Marine battalions at Danang. In June, American troops went into combat for the first time. As the buildup and the bombing continued, Hanoi responded by sending its own regular fighting units down the Ho Chi Minh Trail and into the South.

From this point the ICC declined into almost total desuetude. On occasion Canada sought to revive the Commission as an active supervisory force, but the Indians were usually reluctant and the Poles were always hostile. At different times Ottawa also tried to interest New Delhi and Warsaw in using the Commission as a vehicle to bring the belligerents to the conference table; despite some optimistic and ambiguous statements by Martin, these efforts also came to nothing.

For all the belligerents, the ICC was now little more than a minor embarrassment, a pathetic reminder of the Geneva Agreements which they had all been breaking, almost from the start. As a further humiliation, the Commission was practically broke (for years the Saigon headquarters had been threatened with water and electricity cutoffs because the ICC was almost always late in paying its bills). Each of the three members paid the salaries of its own contingent but the general expenses were supposed to be met by China, the Soviet Union, France and Britain: China had stopped paying its share in 1962. In March 1968, the ICC was forced to make drastic economies, withdrawing all five of its inspection teams in the South and cutting its staff from 450 to 300.*

From then almost nothing more was heard of the ICC, to the point where most Canadians probably forgot its existence. In March 1971, External Affairs Minister Mitchell Sharp admitted the obvious when he stated in a television interview that the Commission had turned into a farce — a fact for which he blamed the Poles and the Indians. In 1972, when India established diplomatic relations with North Vietnam, the Saigon government decided that the Indian delegation should leave South Vietnam. Amid open quarreling between the Canadians, on the one hand, and the Poles and Indians, on the other, the ICC moved its headquarters back to Hanoi.

With the belligerents negotiating a new truce in Paris, it became evident that the ICC would play no part in the settlement. When the Paris Agreement was signed in January 1973, and the first ICCS contingents reached Saigon, the ICC became superfluous. It adjourned *sine die* in February, exhausted from its internal squabbling, ridden with debts and completely unmourned.

* * * * *

In less dramatic fashion, the smaller International Control Commissions in Laos and Cambodia suffered the same fate as the ICC in Vietnam. Both became divided on ideological lines and largely powerless as soon as the conflict spread beyond the borders of Vietnam. This extension of the war was made inevitable by (1) North Vietnam's reliance on the Ho Chi

---

* At its peak — in 1955 and 1956 — the Canadian strength on all three Indochina commissions was 168, consisting of 133 servicemen and 35 civilians. Of this total, 107 Canadians were serving in Vietnam. There were only 18 Canadians on the Vietnam Commission when it was wound up in 1973.

Minh Trail through Laos and Cambodia as its major supply and infiltration route into South Vietnam and (2) American attempts to interdict this route and to deny the Communists their sanctuaries. The political and military struggles within Laos and Cambodia reflected the fortunes and priorities of the antagonists in Vietnam; it was always evident that there would be no lasting settlement in either country until the Vietnam war had been finally resolved.

In Laos — as in Vietnam — the ICC did useful work in supervising the separation and regrouping of the adversaries in the months immediately after the 1954 Geneva settlement. In 1958, with the situation relatively quiet, it was dissolved at the request of the Laotian government. By 1961 renewed fighting among rightists, neutralists and the Communists had aroused such international concern that the Commission was revived and Canadian personnel sent back to Vientiane. Canada was one of 14 nations which convened in Geneva from May 1961 to July 1962 for a conference which laid the basis for a neutral Laos, free of foreign interference, as well as a reconstituted ICC. This settlement soon broke down in the wake of the increasing hostilities in Vietnam. With North Vietnamese units fighting in support of the Communist Pathet Lao and the United States backing the government side with vast economic and military aid — including mercenaries from Thailand and frequent bombing raids on Communist territory — the ICC became locked in the same sort of stalemate it was experiencing in Vietnam. In November 1969, Ottawa began reducing its delegation in Vientiane, citing the Commission's ineffectiveness and Ottawa's austerity squeeze. In June 1974, after a ceasefire and the formation of a new coalition government, Canada withdrew entirely from Laos, although the Commission remained formally in existence.

Cambodia was relatively quiet for nearly a decade following the 1954 Geneva settlement, largely due to Prince

31

Norodom Sihanouk's success in following a non-aligned policy. By 1963, however, it was being sucked into the Vietnam maelstrom, with the North Vietnamese making increased use of infiltration routes through eastern Cambodia and the South Vietnamese launching retaliation raids across the border. For the ICC it was Laos and Vietnam all over again, with the Poles and the Indians rejecting Canadian proposals for investigations of the North Vietnamese infiltration. By 1969, Sihanouk had long broken with the United States and was leaning ever closer to the Communists, especially to the Chinese whom he saw as the ultimate guarantor of Cambodian independence. Scorning Canadian pretensions to impartiality, he accused Ottawa of refusing to recognise "the crimes committed by Canada's allies whenever Cambodia was a victim of American-Saigon forces." In December 1969 — just before his overthrow by a rightwing junta — Sihanouk told the ICC to leave and it was adjourned *sine die.* With Sihanouk in exile in Peking, and fighting spreading between the new government and its leftwing opposition, there were various unsuccessful attempts to revive the ICC in Cambodia, but Canada always maintained that it would not participate unless the Commission's functions were clearly defined and effectively supported.

* * * * *

For Canada, the ICC in Vietnam was always a shaky vehicle on which to mount the brave banners of Quiet Diplomacy and Helpful Fixing. Its mandate was limited in scope and meant to be limited in time: with Diem's refusal to hold elections in 1956, the Commission's task became open-ended in a way the Geneva Conference had not envisaged and for which it had made no provisions. Since the ICC was almost totally dependent on the two Vietnamese governments, it could never function effectively once Saigon and Hanoi became determined to curtail its activities. With the Poles always backing the Communist side and the Canadians usually supporting Saigon and Washington, the troika principle soon became unworkable and the Commission was condemned to endless disputes and frequent deadlock.

But the main problem was never the ICC's failure to achieve unanimity; since the Agreements provided for minority reports, each delegation could publicise its views. With the Indians seeking to avoid committing themselves to either side, the real problem for both the Canadians and the Poles was to obtain a majority for any Commission report or action. It was even more crucial that there was no effective authority to which the ICC could make its reports or to which it could refer its disagreements and difficulties. The Commission was made responsible to the members of the Geneva Conference; in practice it reported to Britain and the Soviet Union, the co-chairmen. Inevitably, London and Moscow reacted as guardians of Western and Communist interests. There were lengthy disputes between the two capitals over the publication of ICC majority and minority reports, often ending with a report being finally released by the side whose interests it served. Since the Geneva Conference had long since dissolved itself, there was no continuing political authority — such as the UN Security Council — which could mediate these differences or strengthen the Commission's mandate.

Other weaknesses became evident in the early months of the Commission's work. The Geneva Agreements failed to give the ICC necessary powers to undertake an effective supervisory role. In particular, the Commission's teams were denied full freedom of movement and were made dependent on the Vietnamese authorities for their transport. Later it became clear that a truce supervisory body was also handicapped if it lacked a formal invitation from all the belligerents: when the Saigon government resumed responsibilities in the South from the French Union High Command,

33

it had no legal obligation to honour the ICC's mandate. Finally, the Geneva Agreements failed to set any time limit on the Commission's work, or to make any provisions for a member's withdrawal.

All these weaknesses were carefully noted in Ottawa. In future, Canadian governments would try — with varying degrees of success — to secure better terms and stronger mandates before committing themselves to other peace-keeping operations. But Ottawa paid much less attention to another fundamental lesson of its ICC experience: the fatal inconsistency between its pretensions to be acting as a fair-minded, independent peacekeeper and its continual support for the American side.

It was not only a case of hawkish Canadian diplomats who were zealous in their pursuit of Communist violations and often blind to the other side's infringements; nor was it only a case of Canadian officers passing military information to their American colleagues. Given the nature of the troika system, such activities were probably inevitable. The Poles were even more blatantly partisan and the Communists doubtless expected little better from us.

No — the real fault always lay with Ottawa. It would have been irresponsible for Canada not to have served initially on the ICC, but it was foolhardy to stay on the Commission after it declined into impotence. It was even worse — much worse — to become little more than an apologist for the Americans as they began to devastate a small but proud nation which they could never dominate.

Yet Ottawa was hamstrung by its ideological conception of the war. From their return to office in 1963, Pearson and Martin gave support and comfort to the Americans — often loudly and publicly. It is important to note that this support was offered willingly and not as a response to American pressures. If the Canadian diplomats on the ICC were obsessed with Hanoi's transgressions, their political masters held

34

equally one-sided views. As John Holmes has stated: "When Mr Martin and others were defending United States motives they were expressing their own convictions and not acting as hired agents."[20]

In speech after speech, Martin in particular argued that the root of the problem was Hanoi's attempts to bring South Vietnam under its control through covert but real aggression. Scorning the view that the war in the South was essentially an internal revolt and insisting that the NLF was nothing but a creature of Hanoi, he was presumably echoing the dispatches of his diplomats on the ICC. In maintaining that the conflict was begun, primarily supported and exclusively directed by the North, both Martin and the Canadians on the spot were ignoring all the evidence to the contrary which was available to any journalist in Saigon.[21]

Dipping into a grab bag of Cold War rhetoric, Martin would specifically compare the Vietnam situation to that of Europe in the late 1940s, when the Western Allies had formed NATO to resist Soviet aggression. In Vietnam the North was carrying out similar aggression under the guise of a war of national liberation; while the "free world" had yet to devise means of dealing with this new form of aggression, it had to be brought under control. Otherwise, he warned, there would be similar Communist aggression in Thailand, Malaysia, perhaps India — not to mention Africa and Latin America. Not even John Foster Dulles would have quarreled with such resounding affirmations of the domino theory.[22]

These convictions help to explain why the Canadian soldiers and diplomats were condemned to stay in Vietnam long after their usefulness was ended. Although Ottawa readily agreed that the ICC was increasingly ineffective, it never regarded this fact as a sufficient reason for a Canadian withdrawal. Since the government identified Communist aggression as the real issue in Vietnam, it thought that Canada had a clear duty to play some part in resisting that aggression

— if only by defending Saigon's interests as best it could on the ICC. As Martin saw it, a Canadian withdrawal would be a victory for the Communists and a stab in the back for Washington.

While Pearson made fewer statements on Vietnam, he also solidly supported the American position. In his most revealing speech he told a New York audience in March 1965 that the whole international community shared a responsibility to assist the United States in its "onerous and ungrateful task" of resisting aggression in Southeast Asia. Pearson, of course, was not implying that Canada was about to send combat troops to Vietnam — he was urging the creation of an even larger and more international peacekeeping force — but he made clear that in his view, Hanoi was entirely to blame for the conflict in the South. As a statement of what was actually happening in Vietnam, this was nonsense. More important, it showed that Pearson was reacting to the war almost entirely in terms of his League of Nations experience in the 1930s and his Cold War experience in the late 1940s. To Pearson the Communist challenge in Vietnam was identical to those of Hitler and Stalin in Europe: Saigon had to be spared the fate of Paris and Prague.

Martin had a similar commitment to collective security which derived from a similar background. As a young MP he had also observed the League of Nations in its futile attempts to resist aggression; in World War Two he had been a Parliamentary Secretary in a government which created Canada's defensive alliance with the United States; in the early years of the Cold War he had led Canadian delegations to the United Nations and was later a member of cabinets which proudly honoured Canada's NATO and NORAD commitments.

In the light of both Pearson and Martin's previous experiences and achievements, their commitment to collective security is easily understood. But the principle was grossly misapplied to Vietnam where it was never a black-and-white case of aggression from the North, where the Communists had largely won the mantle of patriotic nationalists — and even the mantle of Confucian legitimacy — and where the Americans were increasingly regarded as the real aggressors. It is doubtful whether Pearson and Martin had any deep understanding of Asia; they certainly made a major misjudgment in seeing its turmoils in terms of Western history.

Although they gave strong public support to US policies, both Pearson and Martin became increasingly sceptical about Washington's pursuit of a military solution. Faithful to the doctrine of Quiet Diplomacy, they conveyed their concern in private conversations. According to Martin, the earliest expression of Canadian doubts came in the autumn of 1963 — shortly after the Liberals had returned to power — during a ministerial meeting in Washington with Rusk, Defense Secretary Robert McNamara and other senior officials. As Martin recalls the meeting, he argued in favour of a negotiated settlement and then asked the Americans how long they were prepared to go on seeking a military victory over the Communists. Leaning across the table and speaking with great emphasis, McNamara replied: "One thousand years!"[23]

Despite such evidence that Washington was launched on a venture of wild and dangerous irresponsibility, Ottawa continued to believe that American *aims* in Vietnam were laudable, even if American *methods* seemed more and more questionable. In 1965, after the Americans had begun bombing the North and were landing troops in the South, Martin sprang to Washington's defence, claiming that it wanted no wider war and certainly no permanent bases in the South. He also argued that the conflict could only be ended by negotiation, rather than military might. While this was an important qualification, it was not even an implied rebuke of American policy, for he would also add approvingly that the United States was willing to negotiate without preconditions, whereas the North Vietnamese had rejected all such suggestions.

This was at a time — mid-1965 — when President Johnson had already *publicly* imposed conditions which Hanoi could never accept — including a refusal to negotiate directly with the NLF and an insistence on an independent South Vietnam, a goal which was contrary not only to Hanoi's objectives but also to the Geneva settlement and the basic direction of the Vietnamese political struggle since 1945.

Ottawa's advocacy of negotiations was another important reason for keeping Canada on the ICC. If negotiations were desirable — and even inevitable — they still had to be *arranged.* With its access to Hanoi, and its close contacts with Washington, Canada could be the middleman who would bring both sides to the conference table. Increasingly, this was to become Ottawa's major justification for remaining on the Commission.

Yet Pearson — more than Martin — came to believe that the bombing was a hindrance to negotiations and that the Americans needed to be prodded to the conference table. In his famous Temple University speech of April 1965, Pearson won some acclaim by urging the United States to initiate — "at the right time" — a limited pause in the bombing of North Vietnam. Although carefully prepared, this was little more than a diffident aside in the midst of a lengthy speech which strongly confirmed the American view of the war: six times in his speech, Pearson accused North Vietnam of aggression. Even his suggestion of a bombing pause was heavily qualified, since he maintained that there had been great provocation for the air strikes and that Hanoi should be given time to reflect and repent.

Lyndon Johnson was not impressed. When Pearson went to lunch with the President in his Camp David retreat, he was subjected to an arm-swinging, lapel-grabbing diatribe that stopped just short of physical violence, according to Canadian Ambassador Charles Ritchie, who was looking on with horror.[24] Pearson would later proudly maintain that he had

38

gone farther in his Temple speech than any other head of government friendly to the United States had ever gone — especially on American soil — and that this should help to refute the charge that Canada was merely an American satellite that was afraid to speak frankly to its powerful neighbour.[25] Since the Prime Minister's speech had been almost obsequious in its deference to American war aims — "The government and great majority of the people of my country have supported whole-heartedly US peacekeeping and peacemaking *(sic)* policies in Vietnam" — this boast seems more than somewhat pathetic.

Although Pearson's speech hardly deserved the reactions it aroused, it marked an uncharacteristic departure from the strategy of Quiet Diplomacy. Martin, in fact, had seen a draft of the speech in advance and had threatened to resign in an attempt to dissuade Pearson from delivering it. When Martin argued that the speech would destroy Ottawa's credibility in *Hanoi* (by leading the North Vietnamese to believe that Canada was sacrificing its influence in Washington), Pearson replied that he was a political leader, that many Canadians were upset by the American bombings and that he had to say something.[26]

It can be argued that by staying on the ICC, Canada at least retained the right to say *something* to the Americans about Vietnam, since membership gave Ottawa a direct stake in the conflict that was not shared by any of Washington's allies in Europe. Whether it was stated publicly or privately, however, the Canadian case over Vietnam was always a weak one. Rather late in the day, Ottawa became concerned that the Americans were obsessed with military victory to the point where their reckless escalation threatened to involve the Russians and the Chinese in a wider war. Since this was a difference over the means, rather than the end, of the conflict, it was always easy for the Americans to shrug off the diffident expressions of Canadian unease. After all, *they* were the people with a vast army in the South and a sophisticated, world-wide intelligence network. They knew better than anyone else how to prosecute the war — and what risks could be taken. They certainly knew much better than those amiable but rather spineless Canadians with their tiresome qualms about the bombing.

There was never any point telling Lyndon Johnson that he could achieve his goals through moderation instead of brutal force. In the case of Vietnam this wasn't true and Johnson knew it — even if he was increasingly baffled by the continued failure of his military escalation. Ottawa's case would have been more realistic — and therefore stronger — if it had argued that *the goals themselves* were hopelessly and disastrously wrong. This would have meant telling the Americans that by propping up successive Saigon governments with economic assistance and military might, they were merely repeating the mistakes of the French and that there was no way a puppet Western regime could survive after twenty years of revolutionary struggle in Vietnam. In other words, cut bait and quit.

Such advice — whether given publicly or privately — would also have been rejected. But it would have had two great advantages over the nervous equivocations of Pearson and Martin. In the first place, it would have been realistic. In the second, it would have enabled Canada to withdraw from the ICC and to have avoided the further humiliating and compromising entanglements which are the subject of the next three chapters. Instead Ottawa stuck to its simplistic and inaccurate views of the conflict and refused to curtail Canada's growing complicity in Washington's increasingly horrendous war.

Pearson, Martin and their cabinet colleagues are not to be blamed for failing in the early 1960s to anticipate the worst horrors that would result from Washington's stubborn pursuit of victory in Vietnam. It would have been difficult to prophesy such atrocities as My Lai, the bombing of hospitals and other civilian targets in the North and the unparalleled devastation which the Americans were to lavish on the South. Nor could the Canadian leaders have known — at least initially — what the Pentagon Papers later revealed: that the balance of forces in Washington was always heavily in favour of escalation rather than negotiation, that attempts by well-meaning outsiders to mediate would always be received with barely disguised contempt and that it would take a Tet Offensive to force the Americans to the conference table.

But in the early 1960s there was ample evidence that the Americans were blundering their way to defeat in Vietnam, that their massive intervention was based on an awesome misunderstanding of Vietnamese history and Vietnamese aspirations, and that the real threat to peace and security in Southeast Asia came from Washington, rather than Hanoi or Peking. Yet the Canadian government, whatever its private reservations, continued to give broad public support to American objectives and to compromise its pretensions to an independent, peace-seeking foreign policy.

two

It is not at all necessary that the Canadians
either agree or disagree.
What is important is that the Canadian
transmit the message and be willing to
do that and report back accurately
what is said.

Henry Cabot Lodge

The planes were slow and creaky Stratoliners that dated back to World War Two. Owned by a French company and leased to the ICC, they made the milk run twice a week: Saigon, Phnom Penh, Vientiane, Hanoi and back again. Mostly they carried ICC personnel and supplies. As the war raged on, there were sometimes paying passengers: lucky journalists or peace emissaries with rare North Vietnamese visas.

There was wine with dinner but nothing else was fancy about the flights. They lumbered low over the jungle and the rice fields because the Stratoliners with their four propeller-driven engines were not pressurised and because radio guidance was often minimal. The pilots were French — grizzled veterans of colonial days who were never strong on discipline and who flew with a certain Gallic flair that startled a first-time passenger. But the ICC delegates learned to sit back and relax, for the pilots knew every rice paddy along the route and they didn't take many chances. After the Americans started bombing North Vietnam, Hanoi would sometimes turn the planes back — often minutes before they reached the border. But there was only one crash in the whole war — in October 1965, one of the Stratoliners disappeared between Vientiane and Hanoi with three Canadians among the passengers. Nothing more was ever heard of it.

Throughout the war these ICC flights were the only link between Saigon and Hanoi. For Ottawa they provided the

"Canadian channel" which Pearson and Martin would use — first at the behest of the Americans and then on their own initiative — in attempts to arrange negotiations. But these attempts only served to deepen Canadian complicity in Washington's policy of taking the war to the North.

In the spring of 1964, with the Communists on the offensive in South Vietnam, Canada entered a new stage in its involvement in the conflict. From this point its peacekeeping role became less important than its attempts to foster a negotiated settlement, even though these were shrouded in secrecy.

The United States made the first move. Just back from a trip to Saigon, Secretary of State Dean Rusk flew to Ottawa for a meeting with Pearson and Martin on April 30. He was seeking their agreement to open a communications channel between Washington and Hanoi using Blair Seaborn, an experienced diplomat who was about to take up his post as Canada's chief delegate to the ICC. On his return to Washington, Rusk reported on the success of his mission in a cable to Henry Cabot Lodge, the powerful Republican politician and Boston Brahmin who was then US Ambassador in Saigon:

> They (Pearson and Martin) readily agreed that Seaborn should plan to spend much more time in Hanoi than have his predecessors in this assignment. They also accept as part of his mission an effort to establish ready access to and close contact with senior authorities in Hanoi, beginning with Ho Chi Minh . . .

In the same cable Rusk described "some of the matters which we roughed out in Ottawa": a careful mixture of threats and blandishments for Seaborn to convey to Hanoi:

> Seaborn should get across to Ho and his colleagues the full measure of US determination to see this thing through. He should draw upon examples in other parts of the world to convince them that if it becomes necessary to enlarge the military action, this is the most probable course that the US would follow . . .
>
> The North Vietnamese should understand that there are many examples in which the Free World has demonstrated its willingness to live in peace with Communist neighbours and to permit the establishment of normal economic relations between these two systems. We recognize North Vietnam's need for trade, and especially food, and consider that such needs could be fulfilled if peaceful conditions were to prevail.[1]

This was the "carrot-and-stick" policy which President Johnson and his advisers were evolving in a desperate attempt to prevent a complete collapse in South Vietnam by persuading Hanoi to seek a diplomatic settlement. The "carrot" was the promise of trade with the West (it was also to include economic aid); the "stick" was the threat that Washington would carry the war to the North itself. Whether or not the Canadians knew it, the Americans and the South Vietnamese were *already* taking joint offensive action against North Vietnam. Under Operation Plan 34A which had started in February, they were kidnapping North Vietnamese citizens for intelligence information, parachuting sabotage and psychological-warfare teams, launching commando raids from the sea to blow up railway and highway bridges and bombarding North Vietnamese coastal installations.[2] To Ho, a threat to "enlarge the

48

military action" could only mean overt US bombing of his country.

In Washington there was growing support for bombing the North in the hope that this would force Hanoi to reduce guerrilla activity in the South to a level where the weak Saigon government could survive without a full-scale commitment of US combat troops. On March 17 the President had accepted a recommendation from Defense Secretary McNamara and ordered that planning for air strikes should "proceed energetically". The first general bombing plan was approved by the Joint Chiefs of Staff on April 17. At a strategy session in Saigon on April 19 and 20, Rusk, Lodge and Gen. Earle G. Wheeler, the Army Chief of Staff, had developed a broad scenario for the planned escalation. As refined in Washington, this scenario envisaged a series of military and political actions, culminating in US air strikes against the North. One of the earliest political moves would be:

> Intermediary (Canadian?) tell North Vietnam in general terms that US does not want to destroy the North Vietnam regime (and is indeed willing to "provide a carrot") but is determined to protect South Vietnam from North Vietnam.[3] (bracketed material in original)

In a further refinement of this scenario, Lodge cabled President Johnson that

> . . . if prior to the Canadian's trip to Hanoi there has been a terroristic act of the proper magnitude, then I suggest that a specific target in North Vietnam be considered as a prelude to his arrival. The Vietnamese air force must be made capable of doing this, and they should undertake this kind of action. . . .

As Lodge saw it, a Canadian warning to Hanoi would be useful if the scenario ran its full course:

Another advantage of this procedure is that when, as and if the time ever came that our military activities against the North became overt, we would be in a strong moral position with regard to US public opinion, the US Congress, and the UN. I say this because we would then have a record to show that we had given Ho Chi Minh fair warning to stop his murderous interference in the internal affairs of Vietnam.[4]

Wittingly or not, Canada was being dragged into a major US program for expanding the war in which Ottawa was to proffer a very meagre carrot while conveying the threat of an extremely heavy stick. Pearson reaffirmed his government's willingness to help the Americans on May 28, during a New York meeting with Johnson. At the time, this meeting seemed so casual that it was almost ignored by the press: Pearson had gone to New York to speak at a conference of the Iron and Steel Institute and Johnson was in town for a political gathering. At the President's request the two leaders had a 30-minute talk in the Hilton New Yorker Hotel; afterwards Pearson told reporters it had been a "social talk" dealing with such matters as Great Lake problems.

In fact, Johnson had wanted to talk about Vietnam. It was part of a two-pronged effort by the Americans: on the same day William Sullivan, a senior State Department official who was chairman of an inter-agency Vietnam Task Force, was in Ottawa to see Martin, Seaborn and other Canadian officials. If the Pentagon Papers tell the true story, the Pearson-Johnson meeting was one of the most remarkable exchanges in the history of Canadian-US relations. According to this American version, Johnson outlined his Vietnam policy — including the carrot-and-stick aspect — and told Pearson he needed a confidential and responsible interlocutor to carry the message to Hanoi:

Pearson, after expressing willingness to lend Canadian good offices to this endeavor, indicated some concern about this *(sic)* nature of the "sticks". He stipulated that he would have great reservations about the use of nuclear weapons, but indicated that the punitive striking of discriminate targets by careful iron bomb attacks would be "a different thing". He said he would personally understand our resort to such measures if the messages transmitted through the Canadian channel failed to produce any alleviation of North Vietnamese aggression, and that Canada would transmit messages around this framework.

In Ottawa Sullivan found much the same disposition among Canadian officials. While Foreign Minister Martin seemed a little nervous about the prospect of "expanding the war", External Affairs officials readily assented to the use of Seaborn as interlocutor.

Seaborn who struck Sullivan as an alert, intelligent and steady officer, readily agreed to these conditions and has made immediate plans for an accelerated departure. . . .[5]

This report was contained in a cable to Ambassador Lodge in Saigon, signed by Acting Secretary of State George Ball. If accurate, it indicates that Pearson was given advance notice of the US bombing plans and effectively approved them. It suggests that Martin and Seaborn were told *something* about the US escalation scenario and that Martin expressed some doubts. Above all, it demonstrates a degree of Canadian complicity that was never apparent at the time or even later — just the opposite, since Martin and his successor, Mitchell Sharp, were always to claim that Ottawa had no advance knowledge of the air strikes.

Was the report accurate? When it was first published — in 1973 — Pearson was dead and could not reply to the slur on his reputation. Although there is no doubt that the meeting took place, External Affairs officials found no reference to it in their records, nor was there any account of it in Pearson's personal papers. The investigation also indicated that there had been no other Canadian in the room.[6] Many in Canada were quick to spring to Pearson's defence. The *Toronto Star* said in an editorial that there was "no convincing evidence" to support the American report, pointing out that at about the same time, Pearson had told a private gathering he had advised Johnson to get out of Vietnam. Martin said it was "preposterous" to suggest that a Nobel Peace Prize winner could be party to a plan to bomb people. Ball said he had no recollection of the cable, although it might have been drafted by someone else and sent out in his name (this would be normal diplomatic practice, since Rusk was out of the country, Ball was Acting Secretary and the cable was addressed to a senior ambassador). Ball also said he didn't believe that Pearson and Johnson had talked about bombing plans because "there never was any plan at the time they met."[7]

Yet there *was* a plan for bombing the North at the time of the Pearson-Johnson meeting. It had been approved by the Joint Chiefs on April 17. By the end of May there was a list of 94 specific targets. Washington would use this list in early August to order retaliatory air strikes on less than six hours notice during the Tonkin Gulf crisis.[8]

Assuming that Pearson was told about the bombing plans, the American report might have been based on a genuine misunderstanding of his response. The Prime Minister was always anxious to avoid antagonism, confrontation and especially impasse — this was the key to his diplomatic style. Perhaps he was horrified at the idea but instinctively responded in a veiled and ambiguous manner, rather than ruffle LBJ. Yet the cable to Lodge is sufficiently detailed — including the use of direct quotation — to indicate that Pearson's approval of the bombing plan was given without any equivocation, except on the matter of nuclear weapons. It also suggests that one of the Americans was taking notes, or else made a quick summary once Pearson had left the room.

The note-taker was almost certainly McGeorge Bundy, the President's Special Assistant for National Security Affairs. The State Department cable mentions that Bundy was the third man at the meeting: ten years later Bundy confirmed this fact, recalling that he had fetched Pearson from his room in another hotel, guided him through the security guards around the President's suite and then remained for the 30-minute talk. Bundy doubted that there was anyone else at the meeting and assumed that the State Department cable was based on his own notes. Although he had no clear recollection of the conversation, he said there was "no reason to suppose that the cable was not an accurate summary."[9]

There is also indirect confirmation of the report from William Bundy, the older brother of McGeorge who was playing a key role in the Vietnam deliberations in his post as Assistant Secretary of State. Although he was out of the country on the day of the meeting, he easily recalled the context in which it had taken place. There had been an upsurge of fighting in Laos, where North Vietnamese troops were giving strong support to the Communist Pathet Lao. At a high-level strategy meeting on the previous weekend, "the bombing script came back on the table." But Johnson and his advisers were anxious to give the North Vietnamese one last chance to mend their ways, so they seized on Seaborn's forthcoming trip to Hanoi "as an opening shot across their bows". Like his brother, William Bundy had no specific recollection of the cable to Lodge, but he was sure of its authenticity. "There was no reason to fabricate it," he stated. "It was consistent with everything that was happening at the time. It seems iron-clad."[10]

This is all American evidence, without either confirmation or refutation from the Canadian side. But the evidence is strong and detailed: it leads almost inescapably to the conclusion that Pearson *did* have advance knowledge of the plan to bomb North Vietnam and that he *did* approve it. Nor is this really surprising. Although Pearson was a Nobel Peace Prize winner, he was never a pacifist. As a firm believer in collective security, he had been a leading advocate within the cabinet of sending Canadian troops to fight in Korea. In the case of Vietnam, Pearson fully accepted the US view that it had to deter Communist aggression. In May 1964, he was apparently willing to approve US air strikes if Seaborn's mission "failed to produce any alleviation" of that aggression. Most likely he envisaged the bombing as a means of hastening negotiations and avoiding the commitment of US ground troops to the conflict.

Even a year later, when Pearson used his Temple University speech to suggest a pause in the bombing, he did not criticise the strikes in principle. He only became disillusioned with the bombing because the raids were hindering rather than helping the cause of negotiations, because they involved a use of force which was out of all proportion to the provocation and because they carried the threat of dragging the Chinese and the Russians into a wider war. All that was in the future: in the spring of 1964, Pearson saw no reason to object to Johnson's escalation scenario.

It later became obvious, however, that Ottawa and Washington always held sharply different views about Seaborn's role in the scenario. This role was partially revealed in June 1971 when portions of the Pentagon Papers were carried by the *New York Times*. Rejecting opposition charges that Seaborn had been a mere messenger boy for the Americans, Mitchell Sharp told the House of Commons that Seaborn acted as a channel of communication, not as a direct representative of the US government, that the messages were passed via Ottawa and their contents were known to the Canadian government, that Canada did not associate itself with their contents and that Canada was free to add its own comments to any messages passed in either direction. "There were no messages in the sense that the United States instructed us to have any messages carried from them to Hanoi. Mr Seaborn was at all times acting for Canada." To this Martin later added he had told Rusk that Canada would decide what Seaborn should pass on to Hanoi — he would not be allowed to convey any threats or anything that might put Ottawa in an invidious position. For this reason, Martin refused to have Seaborn transmit part of Washington's first proposed message to the North Vietnamese.[11]

For their part, some of the Americans were initially apprehensive about using a foreign intermediary. There was concern in Washington *before* the Pearson-Johnson meeting about giving Ottawa too many details of the scenario. On May 22, William Bundy sent an "Eyes Only" cable to Lodge which read in part:

> In the light of recent Canadian attitudes we tend to see real difficulty in approaching the Canadians at this time with any message as specific as you suggest, i.e. that Hanoi be told by the Canadians "that they will be punished". . . . As you can see, the more specific message might lead us into a very difficult dialogue with the Canadians as to just what our plans really were. . . .

Three days later Lodge trumpeted back in another "Eyes Only" cable to Rusk:

> It is not rpt not at all necessary that the Canadians either agree or disagree. What is important is that the Canadian transmit the message and be willing to do that and report back accurately what is said. . . .[12]

This is a classic example of the arrogance with which the Americans always regarded Canadian attempts to help them reach the conference table. This arrogance may have been unconscious or unintended; it was certainly decisive. It may never have been expressed directly to any Canadian, but it consistently occurred when the Americans were discussing the Seaborn missions with each other. Whatever Ottawa might say or even believe, the Americans regarded Seaborn as a messenger boy to be briefed and dispatched at the whim of Washington. The cool, calculating assumption that Canadians were simply there to be *used* is strikingly evident in an internal State Department paper written by Bundy on November 5, after Seaborn had already made two trips to Hanoi:

> Secretary Rusk is talking today to (Soviet Ambassador) Dobrynin. For more direct communication, Seaborn can be revved up to go up (to Hanoi) on the 15th if we think it wise. He is not going anyway, and we could probably hold him back so that the absence of any message was not itself a signal.

(As it turned out, Seaborn willingly delayed his trip for a week at the Americans' request).[13]

Contrary to Ottawa's assertions that it retained control over Seaborn's messages, another State Department memo prior to the Canadian's first mission stated:

> The interlocutor or his government need not agree with (and) not associate themselves with the messages that are passed. The only requirement is that there be faithful transmission of the messages in each direction.[14]

The assumption that Seaborn was nothing more than a tool of Washington is contained in several other "instructions" for the Canadian envoy — the word is taken from the same internal US document. Throughout these documents there is a further assumption that Seaborn — a highly skilled and perceptive Canadian diplomat — should transmit statements of US policy as his own opinions. In a cable from Rusk to Lodge, it is stated that Seaborn, then preparing for his first trip to Hanoi, "should spread the word that *he* is puzzled by Hanoi's intentions."[15] A later message signed by Under-secretary of State Averell Harriman states that Seaborn should convey to the North Vietnamese leaders an "attitude of real *personal* concern over the growing possibility of direct confrontation between North and South Vietnam."[16] (italics added)

Washington regarded Seaborn as its eyes, ears and mouth in Hanoi. Aside from transmitting US messages, he was instructed to bring back political intelligence on the level of war-weariness among the North Vietnamese, on the state of their economy, on the respective influence of the Russians and the Chinese and on possible divisions among the leaders. While it is obvious that Hanoi would assume that Seaborn would be reporting to Washington on these matters, it is debatable whether the Canadian government should have allowed its envoy to be placed in such a compromising position.

Seaborn received his "instructions" from Washington in early June, just before his departure for Saigon. Aside from the request for political intelligence, he was given a detailed outline of the carrot-and-stick policy to convey to Hanoi. This stressed President Johnson's desire for peace in Southeast Asia and his determination that North Vietnam should end its support for the war in the South. Seaborn was told to emphasise that US patience with North Vietnamese aggression was growing extremely thin; he could also hint at the economic benefits enjoyed by Yugoslavia, Poland and other Communist countries which accepted peaceful coexistence with the West. The instructions included:

In sum, the purpose of Mr Seaborn's mission in North Vietnam would be as an interlocutor with both active and passive functions. On the passive side, he should report either observations or direct communications concerning North Vietnamese attitudes towards extrication from or escalation of military activities. On the active side, he should establish his credentials with the North Vietnamese as an authoritative channel of communications with the US. In each of these functions it would be hoped that Mr Seaborn would assume the posture that the decision as to the future course of events in Southeast Asia rests squarely with Hanoi.[17]

Even if Pearson had failed to tell his colleagues about Johnson's escalation plans, Martin and the senior officials in External Affairs must have realised that the message which Seaborn was carrying to Hanoi could only be interpreted as a threat to start bombing the North. To suggest otherwise would be to imply a level of political naïveté almost beyond imagination. We can be certain, moreover, that when Seaborn left Ottawa for Saigon in June, the Canadian government could have had few illusions about the prospects for his mission — especially the prospect that it might lead to serious negotiations. According to Chester Cooper, a senior US official who accompanied Sullivan to Ottawa for the May 28 meeting with Martin and Seaborn:

Actually we had little of consequence to say. The American bargaining position was just about nil; the South Vietnamese forces were being mauled; there were not enough American advisers in Vietnam to influence the tide of events, but there were more than enough to give us the onus of running the country; opposition to the war was already evident and growing in the United States. Although Seaborn pressed for something nourishing to put before the North Vietnamese, he gracefully accepted the thin gruel he received.[18]

* * * * *

Seaborn's first trip to Hanoi went largely unnoticed in the press and was almost totally ignored in Ottawa where only a few politicians and officials knew that it marked a significant addition to Canada's role in Vietnam. It was routine for a new head of an ICC delegation to pay courtesy calls on both the North and South Vietnamese governments; in Hanoi the Canadians were rarely given access to a senior leader. But on June 18, Seaborn had a 90-minute talk with Prime Minister Pham Van Dong: a meeting which both sides agreed to keep strictly secret.

Seaborn reported on the meeting in two lengthy cables to Ottawa, both of which are included in the diplomatic section of the Pentagon Papers.[19] In Ottawa the cables were passed on to the US Embassy, while Seaborn also reported directly to Ambassador Lodge in Saigon. At the end of his first cable, Seaborn writes: "I expect to be seeing Mr Lodge shortly after my return to Saigon (this tel is being drafted in plane enroute from Hanoi) and will show him copy."

It is clear from the cables that Ottawa had chosen an able man for an extremely difficult assignment. Seaborn was then 40; although new to Asia he had already served as Counsellor in Moscow after earlier postings to Paris and The Hague. Red-haired, slim and of medium height, the Toronto-born diplomat was known to colleagues and journalists as a serious and dedicated professional with a lively mind and a good sense of humour. "A great man for a crisis job," was a typical Ottawa assessment at the time.

In Pham Van Dong, Seaborn was confronting one of Hanoi's most powerful and experienced leaders: a veteran revolutionary who headed the Viet Minh delegation to the 1954 Geneva Conference where he impressed Western delegates with his stubborn persistence in negotiations. Both men spoke in French; according to Seaborn, Dong "took pains

59

throughout interview to give impression of quiet sincerity, of realisation of seriousness of what we were discussing and of lack of truculence or belligerency. Certainly in presence and mental stature PM is head and shoulders above (the) few other North Vietnamese whom I met and undoubtedly an impressive Communist personality by any standards."

The interview began well, even graciously, with Dong telling Seaborn that "he greatly appreciated role Canada had undertaken to play, which he felt was important and desirable, and wished me also personal success in task. From tone of conversation thereafter, I believe Pham Van Dong has understood and accepted and perhaps welcomed my role as intermediary."

Seaborn told the Prime Minister that Canada had close and friendly relations with the United States and an excellent insight into American thinking. The Canadian government was convinced that President Johnson was a man of peace and wanted to avoid any confrontation between the major powers. But he was determined that Southeast Asia should not fall under Communist control through subversion and guerrilla warfare. Then Seaborn conveyed the gist of Washington's carrot-and-stick approach, closely following the points in the State Department's outline.

Although he apparently refrained from relaying any specific threats, Seaborn told Dong that "if conflict in area should escalate, which I did not RPT not think was in anyone's interest, the greatest devastation would of course result for the DRVN* itself." Dong returned to this point later in the conversation, stating that he was glad to hear Washington did not have aggressive intentions and did not intend to attack North Vietnam. This was probably an attempt to draw further information out of Seaborn; significantly, the Canadian decided that he couldn't let it pass:

* DRVN — Democratic Republic of Vietnam: North Vietnam

I corrected him at this point and said USA did not RPT not want to carry war to North but might be obliged to do so if pushed too far by continuation of Viet Minh-assisted pressures in SVN.* I repeated that USA patience was not RPT not limitless.

Seaborn was convinced that Dong understood the importance of his message. The North Vietnamese leader listened carefully and made no attempt to interrupt or disagree, even when Seaborn mentioned Hanoi's complicity in the conflict in the South: a charge which North Vietnam was stoutly denying. In reply, Dong said he had no immediate or specific message for Washington. But he stressed that a "just solution" would depend on an American withdrawal and a negotiated settlement between Saigon and the National Liberation Front which would be based on the NLF's programme for peace and neutrality. If Washington increased its support for Saigon, the war would be prolonged and intensified. "It is impossible for Westerners to understand strength of people's will to resist, to continue, to struggle. It has astonished us, too."

Later Seaborn made a point that was clearly a Canadian, rather than an American view, telling Dong that the NLF would have to participate in any coalition that might emerge, since it represented a "certain force" in South Vietnam, if not a majority of the people, as Hanoi claimed (Washington was firmly opposed to any political role for the Front). Seaborn added: "My fear however was that coalition would soon be taken over by Front as had happened in other countries and that other rep elements would suffer or be ousted. PM merely said there was no RPT no reason to have such fears."

In his second cable Seaborn made a perceptive and painstaking attempt to assess the attitudes of the North

* SVN — South Vietnam

Vietnamese leaders and to meet Washington's request for political intelligence — while stressing that a three-day visit by a newcomer to Asia made such evaluations difficult. He reported that Hanoi was undoubtedly worried by the Sino-Soviet dispute but that it would be wrong to underestimate the unifying strength of national pride. There were no signs of serious divisions among the leaders, nor of malnutrition and sagging morale among the people.

Tentative conclusion is that we would be unwise at this stage to count on war weariness or factionalism within leadership or possible material advantages to DRVN or kind of Asian Tito-ism as of such importance to cause DRVN to jump at chance of reaching accommodation with USA in this area. Certainly on my brief visit I detected no RPT no evidence to suggest (as some columnists have been doing) that starvation, war weariness and political discontent are bringing regime close to collapse and that they would therefore grasp at any straw which might enable them to save something before country falls apart.

Prospect of war being carried to North may give greater pause for thought. But I would hesitate to say that DRVN are yet convinced, despite USA public statements and moves and private msg I have conveyed, that USA really would be prepared to take this step, ultimate consequences of which could be start of World War III. I am also inclined to think that DRVN leaders are completely convinced that military action at any level is not RPT not going to bring success for USA and Govt forces in SVN. They are almost as completely convinced that Khanh Govt is losing ground on political front and are confident that in fullness of time success is assured for Liberation Front supported by DRVN.

This was diplomatic reporting of the highest order. With a cool professional skill, the Canadian was telling Washington that its carrot-and-stick policy simply wasn't going to work. Proud and confident of eventual success, the North Vietnamese would reject the carrot and brace themselves to receive the stick; they were a long way from caving in, or from accepting negotiations on American terms.

We now know that Seaborn was accurate in his perceptions. When the Paris Agreement was finally completed — after nine more years of fighting and thousands more dead — the North Vietnamese had withstood the heaviest sustained bombing that any people had ever suffered. Yet they were strong enough to force Washington not only to withdraw its forces from South Vietnam but also to accept the continued presence of North Vietnamese troops in the South and the existence of the NLF as one of two rival administrations in the country — both of which would remain anathematic to Washington almost to the end.

Tragically, the Americans paid no attention to Seaborn's assessments. In his memoirs President Johnson dismissed the Canadian mission in a few terse sentences:

> Seaborn, an experienced diplomat, presented our views not as an advocate but as a dispassionate intermediary. He listened to the North Vietnamese views in the same spirit. All he heard from Hanoi's leaders was propaganda repeated many times since: The United States should withdraw totally from the South; a "neutral" regime should be set up in accordance with the National Liberation Front's program; the Front would have to take a leading role in the future of the country.
>
> Obviously, the Communist leaders believed they were winning in the South. With things presumably going their way, they had no interests in a peaceful settlement or

63

compromise of any description. They slammed the door shut on our peace offer.[20]

According to Johnson, there was heavy pressure at that point to expand the war, with the Joint Chiefs urging immediate measures against the North and the White House "trying to put on the brake". Shortly after Seaborn's return from Hanoi, the brake was steadily released. In late July, the US sent 5,000 more military advisers to South Vietnam, bringing its total to 21,000. In the same week, Washington instructed its new ambassador to Saigon, Gen. Maxwell Taylor, to tell Gen. Khanh, the embattled South Vietnamese leader, that Washington was considering attacks on North Vietnam.[21] All that the Americans needed was a pretext — and that was soon to come.

* * * * *

On August 2 the US destroyer *Maddox* was steaming in the Gulf of Tonkin, about 30 miles off the coast of North Vietnam. This was a routine intelligence patrol in international waters but the North Vietnamese understandably linked it with the clandestine operations that the South Vietnamese were mounting in the Gulf under American direction as part of Operation Plan 34A: only two nights earlier, South Vietnamese naval commandos had staged an amphibious raid on the North Vietnamese islands of Hon Me and Hon Nieu. When the *Maddox* came on the scene, North Vietnamese torpedo boats were still searching the seas around the islands for the raiders — three of them attacked the *Maddox*. An eyewitness reported that President Johnson "climbed the walls" when he heard of the attack, although American officials concluded that it was a local act of retaliation for the island raids, rather than a premeditated decision taken by Hanoi.[22]

Two nights later the *Maddox* and its sister ship, the *C. Turner Joy*, reported another attack by North Vietnamese vessels. Later there was considerable controversy as to whether the evidence for this second attack was conclusive. But the Pentagon pulled out its list of targets and Johnson approved retaliatory strikes against four torpedo boat bases and an oil storage depot. The President also went on television to tell the nation of his "limited and fitting" response; he then presented Congress with his request (which had also been waiting on the shelf) for wide powers of military action in Southeast Asia. This became known as the Tonkin Gulf Resolution: the Administration regarded it as equivalent to a declaration of war. It was passed on August 7 by a vote of 88 to 2 in the Senate and 416 to 0 in the House of Representatives.*

Within three days the Administration had achieved two key elements in its escalation scenario which dated back to May: the first air strikes against North Vietnam and Congressional authorization for wider action. It was now time to repeat another move in the scenario: on August 10 Seaborn returned to Hanoi to make sure that Pham Van Dong had understood the message of the strikes and the resolution.

Washington had asked Seaborn to assure the North Vietnamese that none of its destroyers had been connected with the raid on the North Vietnamese islands. He was to tell them that Washington's response to the attacks on its destroyers had been limited and fitting. But US public and official patience with North Vietnamese aggression in South Vietnam and Laos was growing extremely thin — as indicated by the fact that the Tonkin Gulf Resolution had been passed with near unanimity. If Hanoi persisted in its present course, "it can expect to continue to suffer the consequences."[23]

* At the time, none of the Congressmen knew about the clandestine raids which apparently provoked the North Vietnamese attacks. Several later charged that they were badly duped by the White House.

With its clear threat of further bombing, this message shows that the Canadian government had been put in an invidious and compromising position — despite Martin's determination that this should never happen. Pearson had already told the House of Commons that he had urged Washington to take no action which would result in further escalation:

> I am quite sure that the US government should limit — as they would desire to limit — their action in this matter to the requirements of the situation and to meeting an attack on their forces, in this case by a Communist dictatorship in North Vietnam.

In effect Pearson was accepting Washington's version of the Tonkin Gulf incident and condoning the US retaliation. On the one hand, the Prime Minister was urging moderation and restraint, while assuring MPs that the Americans "would desire to limit" their actions against North Vietnam. On the other hand, his envoy was warning the North Vietnamese that there *would* be further US attacks unless they abandoned their struggle against Saigon. By this point Canada was deeply and hypocritically implicated in the developing US strategy to extend the war against the North.

Seven years later Mitchell Sharp defended the relay of the American message — "despite its severity" — telling the House of Commons that the Canadian government believed at the time "that because of its importance and in the interests of peace, it should be transmitted faithfully in accordance with our undertaking to the United States." Pressed by opposition members, Sharp refused to concede that Ottawa should have protested to Washington "on the basis of what it is now claimed that it knew about American intentions." According to Sharp:

The Canadian government had no information that would have justified such a protest at the time. Canada, along with many others, accepted the United States government's version of the Gulf of Tonkin incident.

But Ottawa *did* know that the North Vietnamese islands had been attacked (since Washington's message for Seaborn contained a reference to these attacks). This alone should have made Ottawa sceptical of Washington's version. It is also hard to believe that with their diplomatic and military contacts in Saigon, the Canadians did not have some knowledge of the whole programme of clandestine raids against the North which had been carried out for more than six months under Operation Plan 34A. As for "American intentions", the US message for Seaborn could have left Ottawa in no doubt that these included further bombing of the North.

It is hardly surprising that Seaborn received an "angry reaction" from Pham Van Dong when he delivered the American message on August 13. The Prime Minister told him:

The Government of the USA is obliged to carry out aggression against us. Official circles both political and military have decided that it is necessary to carry the war to the North in order to find a way out of the impasse in which they find themselves in the South. . . .[24]

Apparently Dong had a much clearer idea of Washington's intentions than did the Canadian government which — according to Sharp — *still* remained ignorant of any US plan to bomb the North. Dong also told Seaborn that the situation was very dangerous. "If the war comes to North Vietnam, it will come to the whole of Southeast Asia. We do not hide the fact that the people will have to make many sacrifices, but we are in a state of legitimate defence because the war is imposed upon us."

Assessing this conversation in a cable to Ottawa,[25] Seaborn speculated that despite Johnson's reassurances, the North Vietnamese might be expecting further American strikes even if they did nothing to provoke them. "They are at least acting as if this were their estimate and are taking various precautionary measures (air raid drills, slit trenches, brick bunkers, etc and reportedly at least preparation for evacuation of women and children)."

While Dong gave no indication of being worried by the firmness of the American warning, Seaborn found it mildly encouraging that he calmed down in the course of their conversation and significant that he clearly stated he wanted to keep the Canadian channel open. But Seaborn again warned Washington that Dong seemed genuinely convinced that things were bound to go his way in Indochina and that there was no need to seek compromises. For this reason Seaborn saw little chance that Hanoi would use the Canadian channel — "for some time at least" — to send any new proposals to Washington.

Again Seaborn's assessment was accurate. In the months ahead Hanoi showed little interest in reaching negotiations with the Americans. According to President Johnson, the North Vietnamese "slammed the door even harder" on Seaborn in August than they had in June. "We could only conclude from his experience that the North Vietnamese had no desire to limit their actions or to negotiate; they were interested in only one thing, victory on the battlefield."[26]

The Americans were equally intransigent. In South Vietnam they were facing continuing Communist military victories and continuing political instability in Saigon, where the government was being reshuffled almost on a monthly basis. While these two factors limited Washington's ability to manoeuvre, Johnson's landslide victory over Barry Goldwater in the November election seemed to give him more elbow room, since the electorate had overwhelmingly rejected the

Republican candidate and his hawkish views. Although there was a great deal of talk in Washington about "reconsidering" the whole situation, however, the Administration remained firmly opposed to any accommodation with the Communists that would allow the NLF to play a part in the South's postwar politics.

* * * * *

With grim inevitability the United States and North Vietnam were moving steadily toward a wider war. Neither side had much to say to the other; as Seaborn prepared to make a third trip to Hanoi in December, the Americans had little to offer him. In a cable to the US Embassy in Saigon, Harriman outlined the State Department's latest message to Ottawa:

> Canadians are asked to have Seaborn take the following position during his next visit to Hanoi. . . .
>
> The United States has nothing to add to the points made by Seaborn on his last visit to Hanoi in August. All the recent indications from Washington, however, point to a continued and increasing determination on the part of the US to assist the South Vietnamese in their struggle. Although he has no specific message on this trip, Seaborn has noted from its public statements increased US concern at DRV role in direct support of Viet Cong, and this together with reported high-level meetings Washington makes him feel that time is ripe for any new message Hanoi may wish to convey.
>
> Seaborn should convey attitude of real personal concern over growing possibility of direct confrontation between GVN* and DRV.
>
> FYI: Purpose of this approach is to probe for any new DRV reactions.[27]

* GVN — Government of Vietnam: South Vietnam

This was still the carrot-and-stick policy, but with a growing emphasis on the stick (Hanoi would not miss the point of those "high-level meetings"). By now Seaborn was showing some discomfort in his role of messenger for the policy. In early November he had told the Americans in Saigon that the general theme of their last two messages was just about played out; if the Americans had anything for his next trip he hoped it would be something specific. He added that Ottawa had "strongly endorsed" this point.[28]

Seaborn must have been disappointed by the lack of any new American proposals; he found the North Vietnamese equally unforthcoming when he reached Hanoi on December 3. This time there was no meeting with Pham Van Dong: the Canadian had to be content with Col. Ha Van Lau, another veteran of the Geneva Conference who was head of North Vietnam's liaison mission to the ICC. Seaborn reported to Ottawa that Lau did not comment directly on any part of the American message. "Notes were taken throughout," he added somewhat plaintively, "and I assume higher authorities will be informed."

Deprived of any real contact with the North Vietnamese leaders, Seaborn was forced to scrounge around Hanoi's small diplomatic community for scraps of information. Judging from his report to Ottawa, the possibility of American bombing was a favorite topic of conversation:

> Foreign reps with whom I spoke all referred to DRVN concern over possibility of USA air strikes, though there was differing interpretation as to how likely DRVN thought this to be. None seemed to expect anything of a serious nature to be imminent. To those who tended to play down likelihood, I cautioned against complacency and said I did not RPT not rule out possibility of air strikes in retaliation for growing DRVN complicity in SVN insurgency. I detected during this visit to Hanoi

none of tension (partly officially inspired, partly genuine) which was so evident in mid-Aug just after Gulf of Tonkin incident. Nor, as already reported, is there any sign of renewed digging of air-raid shelters or widespread drilling of militia. . . .[29]

This report again raises the question: how much did Seaborn — and Ottawa — know about Washington's detailed plans to start bombing the North, given another suitable pretext? Although Canadian officials later denied any such foreknowledge, the American messages which Seaborn carried to Hanoi in June, August and December all indicated a clear *intention* to bomb unless the North Vietnamese stopped supporting the PLA. The Pentagon Papers also establish that Ottawa was told *something* about the bombing scenario around the time that Seaborn was making his December trip. On December 1, Johnson approved in principle a two-phase bombing plan. In Phase One there would be 30 days of air strikes against infiltration routes in Laos and one or two reprisal raids against the North. Phase Two would introduce a "continuous program of progressively more serious air strikes" against the North for two to six months, during which Hanoi was apparently expected to yield.[30]

It then became a matter of informing America's allies. According to one part of the Pentagon Papers, Britain, Australia and New Zealand received the "full picture" of US intentions, while the Canadian government was told "slightly less". The Philippines, South Korea and Nationalist China were briefed on Phase One only.[31] Another section gives a slightly different version:

Several allies, including the UK, Canada, Australia and New Zealand, were given a fairly complete description of US intentions. Others, such as Thailand and Laos, were informed about Phase I only. Still others, like Nationalist

71

China, Korea and the Philippines, were simply given a vague outline of the projected course of action.[32]

Both versions indicate that Ottawa was given some advance warning of Phase Two which would see American bombers strike progressively farther north of the 17th parallel. Even if Johnson *hadn't* told Pearson about the bombing plans as far back as May 28, Washington's official briefing would have confirmed what Ottawa must have already deduced from the US messages for Seaborn. According to one well-placed American source, the briefing was given by William Bundy to Canadian Ambassador Charles Ritchie in early December. As with the Pearson-Johnson meeting, there was no Canadian objection to the bombing plan.[33]

Yet in June 1971, Sharp assured the House of Commons that during this period Canada did not know of any US intention to bomb North Vietnam. He would only state that "the messages we carried were couched in general terms and related to the possible consequences for the North Vietnamese government of continued activities in South Vietnam."

At any rate, Seaborn was warning foreign diplomats in Hanoi in early December not to discount the possibility of such air strikes. When the bombings started two months later — in response to the PLA attack on Pleiku airbase — Seaborn in his ICC capacity wrote the Canadian minority report which described them as a response to North Vietnam's aggression in the South.

From that point Seaborn's trips to Hanoi became increasingly unproductive. There is no direct evidence that he had lost his credibility with the North Vietnamese leaders but a great deal of evidence that Hanoi was adamant against any negotiations with the Americans while the bombings continued — as Seaborn had predicted.

Reporting to Ottawa on his fourth visit to Hanoi in early March, Seaborn said he had again only managed to see Col.

Lau and that Lau's comments were so unremarkable that Seaborn was sending them by diplomatic bag, instead of by cable. It is not surprising that Lau showed scant interest in the conversation: once again Seaborn had little to offer. The Americans had given him the text of a US statement to the Chinese at their ambassadorial talks in Warsaw. Col. Lau said the statement contined nothing new; besides, he added, the Chinese had already reported to Hanoi on the Warsaw meeting. By this time Seaborn was a messenger boy whose messages were second-hand and stale; it is no wonder that Hanoi was receiving him with barely disguised boredom. As Seaborn told Ottawa:

My personal opinion is that in present circumstances, DRVN have very little interest in (Canadian) channel of communication with USA. They have never taken initiative to use it and this time were not RPT not even sufficiently interested for me to see PM. . . .[34]

Seaborn was also asked by Washington to convey the threat — which was obvious in the face of the air strikes then taking place — that Hanoi now faced "extensive future destruction of . . . military and economic investments" if it did not call off its support for the war in the South.[35] But the North Vietnamese were not impressed by this warning, as Seaborn told Ambassador Taylor in Saigon, who passed on his assessment in a cable to Rusk:

. . . Seaborn also discussed his general impression on which he is drafting separate report. Because of his inability to see any senior official or have any substantive discussion with any Vietnamese, and discussions with Eastern bloc diplomats, primary impression is that Hanoi thus far not seriously concerned by strikes, it being Hanoi's interpretation of events that strikes are only a limited attempt by US to improve its bargaining position for conference which USG is strenuously seeking in order to extricate itself from war in SVN which USG now recognises is lost. Thus Hanoi not very concerned by strikes which have not seriously hurt it and as USG is one urgently seeking conference it is to Hanoi's advantage to continue to hold back on agreeing to any conference which at this time could only, as in 1954, result in depriving DRV of that full victory which it sees in sight as turmoil in SVN continues and pressures on US for withdrawal continue to mount.[36]

In the face of this impasse — and in response to a call for immediate negotiations by 17 non-aligned nations — President Johnson made a major speech at Johns Hopkins University on April 7 in which he said that the US was ready for "unconditional discussions" and offered an American contribution of $1-billion to an international postwar aid programme for Southeast Asia. This was the biggest carrot of them all, but Hanoi remained sternly unimpressed, especially since Washington was still refusing to negotiate with the NLF. The Americans had also just landed two Marine battalions at Danang — the first US fighting units committed to the conflict. To Hanoi this hardly seemed an assurance of Washington's desire for peace. One week after Johnson's speech, the North Vietnamese released their own Four Point peace plan:

(1) The United States must withdraw its troops, weapons and bases from South Vietnam and cease its "acts of war" against North Vietnam.
(2) Pending reunification, both North and South Vietnam must agree that no foreign bases or troops will be allowed on their soil and that they will join no military alliances.

(3) The internal affairs of South Vietnam must be settled in accordance with the program of the National Liberation Front.

(4) The reunification of Vietnam must be settled by the Vietnamese themselves without outside interference.

This proposal was rejected by the Americans who described the Four Points (especially Point Three) as a blueprint for a Communist takeover. But the Administration was coming under growing pressure from peace groups and some Congressmen who wanted a pause in the bombing so that Hanoi's intentions could be further tested. The President ordered a pause on May 13; it lasted five days without any discernable response from North Vietnam.

In the wake of these unpromising developments, Seaborn returned to Hanoi in early June, meeting the North Vietnamese Foreign Minister, Nguyen Duy Trinh, but again hearing nothing new. Trinh told him that Washington's offer of unconditional negotiations was deceitful, since the US was continuing its military buildup in the South and its bombing of the North. Returning to Saigon, Seaborn told the US Embassy that Hanoi was still not interested in negotiations.[37]

Seaborn made one more trip to Hanoi — his sixth — between September 30 and October 4. As Sharp told the House of Commons seven years later, the Canadian envoy carried no message from the Americans and only saw junior officials. Again he detected no sign of any interest in discussions or negotiations with Washington.

At this point the Americans were bombing targets north of Hanoi; they also had nearly 150,000 troops on the ground in South Vietnam. Their commander, Gen. William Westmoreland, was asking for twice that number, while boasting that his search-and-destroy operations would defeat the enemy by the end of 1967. Civilian authorities, including Defense Secretary McNamara, were starting to have serious doubts about the effectiveness of both the ground and air wars, but they continued to recommend escalation as the only acceptable policy. It was no time for peacemakers, Canadian or otherwise, and the Seaborn missions ended on a note of sad futility.

* * * * *

During the long history of the Vietnam conflict, the period from the summer of 1964 to the autumn of 1965 was especially crucial, since it saw the United States take the plunge into another major war on the Asian mainland. While appearing at the time to stumble from crisis to crisis, the Americans were in fact implementing a scenario which was frequently revised but which always had one basic goal: to force Hanoi to negotiate on American terms through the steady application of military pressure. Like a compulsive gambler who can never accept his losses and go home, the United States was soon committing thousands of bombers and hundreds of thousands of troops to this impossible task.

Throughout this period the Canadian channel to Hanoi remained open and frequently in use. Especially in the early stages both sides saw some point in using the channel to signal their intentions to each other. Both sides also loudly maintained their deep desire for a peaceful settlement — always, of course, on their own terms. But it is now clear that *neither* side ever had any intention of using the Canadian channel to start negotiations.

Hanoi was more honest about this than Washington. On Seaborn's first trip, Pham Van Dong agreed to accept the Canadian as an intermediary and listened carefully to the US message. But Dong made clear that he had nothing to offer in return and that he saw little prospect for negotiations. On Seaborn's second visit — just after the Gulf of Tonkin incident — Dong was both angry and adamant; Seaborn drew the obvious conclusion that there was little chance of the

76

North Vietnamese using the Canadian channel to make any new proposals to the Americans. From that point Hanoi showed a steadily declining interest in the Canadian's visits; if it had not been for Seaborn's position on the ICC, the North Vietnamese might well have told him not to waste their time.

Hanoi had good reason to be wary and sceptical of the whole negotiating process. The North Vietnamese felt they had been betrayed in 1946 by the French, who had opened hostilities after an agreement had been reached. They were convinced that both their adversaries and their allies had ganged up on them at Geneva in 1954, forcing them to accept much less than they felt they had earned. Also with good reason, they saw nothing in Washington's offers to allay their suspicion of negotiations: according to Chester Cooper, a White House aide who was closely involved in these diplomatic initiatives, "many of Washington's plans for a 'political solution' involved, for all practical purposes, a negotiated surrender by the North Vietnamese."[38]

Far from contemplating surrender, Hanoi was confident of eventual victory. As Seaborn noted on his first visit, the North Vietnamese were convinced that not even the Americans, with all their money and military muscle, could prevail in South Vietnam in the face of the chronic weaknesses of successive Saigon governments and the growing opposition to the war back in the United States. The Hanoi leaders were under no illusions about the suffering and destruction that Washington could bring to the North itself, but they were willing to pay the cost in order to achieve their goals.

The Americans were following a more devious strategy. Throughout this period the Administration consistently balanced *deeds* of military escalation with *declarations* of political moderation. To give two key examples: the decision to bomb the North in February 1965 was followed by a US appeal to the United Nations; in the following month Johnson sent the first US combat troops to the South and then called for negotiations and offered economic aid in his Johns Hopkins speech. The Americans always maintained that (1) they wanted negotiations, (2) they were willing to negotiate without conditions and (3) the North Vietnamese were preventing a settlement by stubbornly insisting on their Four Points. At the time most of America's allies, including Canada, accepted and supported this position.

It is certainly true that the North Vietnamese were sticking to their Four Points, despite occasional hints that these might be modified. But the rest of the American position was based on deliberate deception. It was always a plain lie that Washington was willing to negotiate "without conditions" since the Americans consistently refused to negotiate with the NLF or to contemplate any role for the Front in South Vietnam's postwar politics. This was a very major condition to Hanoi since there was always one main issue in the war: who should rule in Saigon. By excluding the Front, the Americans were calling for a Communist surrender.

Furthermore the balance of forces in the Administration in 1964 and 1965 was strongly in favor of escalation rather than negotiation. According to David Kraslow and Stuart H. Loory, two American journalists who made a thorough study of the period, Washington was determined to *avoid* negotiations until it had applied much more military pressure on the enemy. "Particularly during the latter half of 1964 and early 1965, those running the war equated negotiations with surrender. The South Vietnamese regime, and thus the American bargaining position, was that weak." According to one State Department policy-maker: "The moment we moved toward negotiations at that stage, it would have been an admission that the game was up."[39]

The Pentagon Papers support this analysis, pointing out that in the spring of 1965, with the American bombings underway, Rusk conducted "a marathon public-information campaign" which "sought to signal a seemingly reasonable but in fact quite tough US position on negotiations. . . ." The Pentagon account continues:

> Rusk's disinterest in negotiations at this time was in concert with the view of virtually all of the President's key advisers, that the path to peace was not then open. Hanoi held sway over more than half of South Vietnam and could see the Saigon government crumbling before her very eyes. The balance of power at this time simply did not furnish the US with a basis for bargaining and Hanoi had no reason to accede to the hard terms that the US had in mind. Until military pressures on North Vietnam could tilt the balance of forces the other way, talk of negotiation could be little more than a hollow exercise.[40]

This official analysis destroys one of the strongest myths of the Vietnam conflict: that the Americans were genuinely willing to negotiate a settlement in the mid-1960s and that only Hanoi's intransigence forced Washington to extend the war. Another strong myth still prevails which has worked its way into much of the literature on Vietnam and is also used to condone Canadian support for US policies. This is the so-called quagmire thesis: the theory that successive American Presidents, from Truman to Johnson, stumbled into a deepening military impasse in Southeast Asia because they were misled by faulty intelligence and optimistic military advice and genuinely believed at every stage that just one more act of escalation would be sufficient to turn the tide against the Communists. According to this myth, the Presidents — especially Kennedy and Johnson — were men of peace who sank their country ever further into the quicksands of Vietnam because they had no idea that victory was always unattainable at acceptable costs and risks.

This myth has also been demolished, most notably by Daniel Ellsberg, who had access to the whole Pentagon Papers in his role as government consultant. According to Ellsberg, the image of successive Presidents "stumbling-into-quicksand" cannot be maintained since government documents show that each received *realistic* military and intelligence estimates. These estimates consistently held that the tide might be turned, but only if the United States took military actions which were always much larger than any President was willing to contemplate at the time. Instead, each President took smaller steps while being warned by his advisers that these wouldn't be sufficient and would eventually demand either further escalation, or else retreat. Each President knew that his actions would almost certainly involve even greater costs in the future, without any significant hope of eventual success. But each plunged deeper into war — *quite deliberately* — in order to preserve the stalemate and buy time through an over-riding fear of retreat or defeat which would resound against his party at the next election. This was especially true for Kennedy and Johnson who were trapped by the anti-Communist rhetoric of American politics and who feared that a Communist victory in Vietnam would be interpreted by the Republicans as another US defeat in the Cold War, equivalent to the "loss" of China by the Democrats, and even as the basis for charges of deliberate treachery.[41]

All this evidence makes clear that the Canadian channel to Hanoi could *never* have been used to arrange peace talks in the crucial years of 1964-1965. Seaborn was conveying American ultimatums which the North Vietnamese could never have accepted and which they were never *meant* to accept. He was taking back statements of North Vietnamese intransigence and defiance which were no different from those being broadcast by Radio Hanoi.

But the Americans saw the Seaborn trips in the larger context of their escalation scenario. They had no hope that Hanoi would suddenly agree to American surrender terms. At the very least, however, Seaborn's missions could serve to rally the faint-hearted in the Administration by giving direct evidence of North Vietnam's stubborn refusal to capitulate. As Lodge suggested, they might also be useful as a public relations exercise — to show at some future date that Washington had given Ho Chi Minh fair warning of its intentions. It seems likely that their main purpose — which was possibly unconscious in many Administration minds — was merely to provide a small gesture of moderation in the midst of a scenario which was otherwise totally directed toward the steady application of military might. In this sense Seaborn provided a sop to the consciences of Johnson and his advisers.

While Seaborn's reports made clear that North Vietnam was confident of withstanding US air strikes, there is no evidence that these reports caused any reassessment of Washington's position. In fact, the only time the Pentagon Papers indicate a direct US response to the Canadian's views involved yet another extension of the conflict. In a cable to Washington after Seaborn's fourth visit to Hanoi, Gen. Taylor noted that the Canadian had found "a mood of confidence" among the North Vietnamese leaders and an absence of concern about the air strikes which had been started in the previous month. He added: "Our objective should be to induce in DRV leadership an attitude favourable to US objectives in as short a time as possible in order to avoid a build-up of international pressure to negotiate." Therefore, he went on, it was necessary to "begin at once a progression of US strikes north of the 19th parallel in a slow but steady ascending movement" to dispel any illusions in Hanoi. The next bombing raids — on March 14 and 15 — were the heaviest in the war to that time, involving 100 American and 24 South Vietnamese planes against barracks and depots on Tiger Island off the North Vietnamese coast and the ammunition dump near Phuqui, 100 miles southwest of Hanoi. For the first time, planes used napalm against the North.[42]

On at least one occasion, Washington also used Seaborn's reports to reject outside attempts to bring about negotiations. In the late summer and autumn of 1964, United Nations Secretary-General U Thant made persistent efforts to bring both sides to the conference table, maintaining that the Russians had told him Hanoi was definitely interested. But Adlai Stevenson, Washington's chief UN delegate, assured U Thant that the North Vietnamese had no desire to negotiate — citing Seaborn's reports as evidence. According to President Johnson, the Secretary-General's approach was "rejected by the United States since the latest report of Blair Seaborn indicated that Hanoi was not prepared for serious talks to end its aggression in South Vietnam. Hanoi later denied that it had suggested any negotiations to U Thant."[43]

* * * * *

It is now clear that the Canadian government allowed itself to become much more intimately involved with the US policy of *avoiding* negotiations and increasing military actions than was ever apparent at the time. Seaborn was used by the Americans to play a small but crucial role in their escalation scenario. The Administration seized on his reports as proof that the North Vietnamese would only negotiate if military pressure was increased, but it ignored his evidence that Hanoi would refuse to surrender, even under heavy bombing.

It has been argued that Canada should have withdrawn from the ICC before 1964. If this had happened, there would have been no Canadian channel to Hanoi and no approach from Washington to carry its messages. Given the fact that Canada remained on the ICC, Ottawa was probably right at least to consider Washington's request. As the Western member of the Commission, and a close ally of the United States in other parts of the world, Canada was a logical choice to convey American messages to the North Vietnamese.

But Ottawa should have had serious doubts about accepting this new role once it became clear that the Americans were bent on military victory rather than a negotiated compromise, and that Seaborn would only be conveying threats and ultimatums. This should have been evident to Pearson on May 28 and to Martin when he received the text of Washington's first message. It certainly must have been evident by the time of the Gulf of Tonkin incident and the American reprisal raids. If Ottawa had paid sufficient attention to Seaborn's reports from Hanoi, it would have realised that the North Vietnamese had no interest in accepting the American surrender terms, that American goals involved a policy of high risk and that this policy had scant chance of success. Yet the Canadian government continued to acquiesce in the US policy by allowing Seaborn to continue in his role as intermediary.

Nor was Ottawa influenced — as it should have been — by the fact that Hanoi soon lost interest in the Canadian channel and regarded Seaborn's visits with increasing indifference. This was evident on his third trip in December 1964, when he was given only veiled threats to convey to the North Vietnamese. On his fourth trip in the following March he was asked to convey the specific threat of "extensive further destruction". At that point Seaborn had ceased to be a dispassionate intermediary (Johnson's phrase) and had become a virtual spokesman for the American policy.

Seaborn, of course, was only acting on instructions. By allowing Canada to be compromised in this way, the government made a major political misjudgment. Martin and Sharp were disingenuous when they later argued that Ottawa had always kept control over Seaborn's messages and was never given advance knowledge of US bombing plans. This would mean — at worst — that Canada was *used* by the Americans and that the government might be accused of naïveté but could never be convicted of complicity.

Yet there *was* complicity. It is almost certain that Pearson was told about the bombing plans at his meeting with Johnson in May 1964 and did not demur. On his first trip to Hanoi in June, Seaborn made a special point of warning Pham Van Dong that Washington might carry the war to the North. After the American bombings which followed the Tonkin Gulf incident in August, Seaborn delivered another clear threat of further raids. In December, Ottawa was given an official briefing on the revised bombing scenario. In plain language, the Canadian government knew from the start that the Americans were planning to bomb the North and was never given any chance to forget this fact.

By allowing Seaborn to carry US ultimatums to Hanoi, the government accepted an active role in the unfolding of this escalation scenario. Once the bombings had begun, Ottawa tried to excuse them by again harping on North Vietnam's aggression in the South. At that time — and later — Pearson and Martin urged restraint on *all* the belligerents and warned against further escalation. But these were little more than pious asides in speeches that bristled with anti-Communist rhetoric and gave strong support to US objectives. Nothing that Pearson and Martin ever said to the Americans — publicly or privately — can mitigate the charge that Canada became an active accessory to Washington's expansion of the conflict.

There was only one thing missing: Canadian troops fighting side-by-side with the Americans. Dean Rusk would later imply — in his usual patronising manner — that Canada's role on the ICC justified the fact that it had not sent combat troops to Vietnam. Some Canadian officials would argue in private that all our frustrations as peacekeepers were worthwhile because they saved the government from a direct American request for military assistance. As one official put it: "Membership on the ICC was our chastity belt against LBJ."

But LBJ had no cause to twist our arms: by 1965 Canada was effectively allied with the United States in its war against North Vietnam. Canadian officials were carrying American ultimatums to Hanoi, arguing America's case on the ICC, furnishing America with political and military intelligence and publicly supporting American policies in Southeast Asia. Canada was also selling about $300-million worth of arms and ammunition to the Americans each year: a large if undisclosed portion of this military hardware was being used in Vietnam. Canadian troops would have almost been superfluous.

Needless to say, Ottawa was never easy in this role of semi-declared ally. For Pearson and Martin, peacemaking was always an instinctive response — especially to a war that now carried the serious threat of a direct confrontation between the Americans and the Chinese, and possibly the Russians. But when Ottawa began to take its own diplomatic initiatives in early 1966, it soon ran afoul of Washington's ruthless determination to win the war at almost any cost.

three

I personally talked to Paul Martin about Ronning and
emphasised that it was extremely important
that Ronning do nothing to encourage a Hanoi
miscalculation about our determination and do
nothing to undermine the publicly stated positions
of the United States. Martin assured me that he
would make that very clear to Ronning. . . . Quite
frankly, I attach no importance to his trip and
expect nothing out of it.

Dean Rusk

Chester Ronning is a large man who walks through the world with long, confident strides, leaving legends in his wake. Tall and erect, with a great shock of white hair and a sharp profile which recalls his Norwegian ancestors, he was always something of an odd-man-out among diplomats. Although his manner is courtly, he rarely tries to hide his opinions, which are often passionate.

Ronning feels deeply about Asia and especially about China, where he was born and where his missionary parents are buried. As the Canadian Charge d'Affaires in Nanking when the Communists came to power in 1949, he urged speedy recognition of the new government and was disappointed when Ottawa hesitated until recognition was ruled out by the Korean War. Fluent in Mandarin, he made a point of having friendly conversations with the Chinese at the 1954 Korean Conference in Geneva where they were rudely snubbed by the Americans. The Chinese never forgot his courtesy, or his diplomatic skills. While Canadians in China during the 1960s were always greeted in the name of Norman Bethune, they often heard Foreign Ministry officials speak with special admiration of Chester Ronning.

After a distinguished career in External Affairs (Ambassador to Norway and High Commissioner to India), Ronning retired in 1965. As a private citizen, he became even more outspoken, especially in advocating Canadian recognition of

89

China. But his career was far from ended. In the winter of 1965-1966, still agile and sharp-witted at the age of 71, Ronning was about to undertake his most difficult diplomatic assignment.

It was a time of great furor in Washington. The Administration was under mounting pressure from peace groups and influential Senators who were urging stronger efforts to end the war; it was also embarrassed by charges that it had sabotaged a mission to Hanoi by Giorgio La Pira, the Italian Christian Democrat. In response President Johnson launched a loud and energetic peace offensive in December, dispatching flocks of high-level emissaries to capitals in every continent. Diplomats cautioned that the Communists would reject any approaches made with such a deafening fanfare, while critics charged that the President was more concerned with his domestic and international public relations than with serious moves to negotiation. But hopes were raised when a Christmas bombing pause was allowed to continue and a Pentagon spokesman acknowledged that the pause was for diplomatic reasons.

The pause lasted 37 days without any clear response from Hanoi. Critics later claimed that there had been *some* response, although this was admittedly muffled and ambiguous. Even the Administration acknowledged a marked decline in Communist military activity, but it chose to ignore this possible sign by landing 11,000 more troops in South Vietnam during the pause. By late January the President was holding long meetings with his military advisers; reports from Washington indicated that the bombing was soon to be resumed.

On January 31, American planes again attacked North Vietnam. Three days earlier, Hanoi had made a resumption almost certain by broadcasting the text of a letter from Ho Chi Minh to the leaders of several nations, including Canada. Ho ridiculed the American peace offensive, pointing out that Washington was frantically increasing its strength in South Vietnam, and again insisted that Washington accept his Four Point Plan. To Johnson, Ho's rejection and scorn were decisive; for two more years he would refer again and again to the fruitless pause, especially whenever anyone suggested another bombing halt. Soon Johnson was disclaiming any desire for further escalation, but pledging to send more troops if his commanders needed them. The big peace offensive was giving way to an even bigger war.

In this dangerous situation, Canada was still giving solid support to the United States. In a speech on January 20, Pearson had described the American peace offers as genuine and sincere. In the House of Commons on January 25, Martin again condemned North Vietnamese aggression and warned that the failure of US efforts in South Vietnam could mean the spread of Communism as far as Australia. On the day the bombing was resumed, Pearson carefully refrained from either criticising or endorsing the American action. He informed the House that he had told the US Ambassador the Canadian government "regrets that in the eyes of the United States government a resumption of the bombing is necessary." There was no attempt to suggest that Washington's view might be askew — just the opposite since Pearson referred to his letter from Ho in order to echo the American contention that North Vietnam was still completely intransigent about entering into negotiations. Pressed by sceptical New Democrats, Pearson retorted: "Mr Speaker, I hope we will do all we can to bring about a negotiated settlement, but that does not include irresponsible statements in this house in criticism of the United States."

Both Pearson and Martin were now doubtful that the bombing would ever force Hanoi to negotiate, but they had no intention of stating this publicly. Ignoring all the growing evidence that Washington was only willing to negotiate a North Vietnamese surrender in the South, they continued to believe that Quiet Diplomacy by Canada might yet bring both sides to the conference table. With the ending of the bombing pause, however, it was obvious that there would be no further initiatives from Washington for some time. In this unpromising atmosphere, Ottawa was soon stirring with intimations of a new Canadian peace move.

With Pearson keeping in the background, it seemed that Martin was making all the running: an impression which induced a certain scepticism among many in the capital. While Martin's devotion to peace was unquestionable, he was always an extremely ambitious politician — much more openly so than Pearson, to whom he had lost the contest to succeed St Laurent in 1957. Inevitably most Ottawa commentators linked his peace initiatives to his personal ambitions. According to Peter C. Dobell, Martin believed that Pearson owed his convention victory to his Nobel Peace Prize:

> Hoping to succeed Pearson as Prime Minister when he retired, Martin could be excused for feeling that international achievements would help him in his goal. So he attempted to overcome public frustration by a desperate search for new successes in traditional areas of policy, an approach which he executed with tactical brilliance, but without having the good fortune of achieving any spectacular results.[1]

There was also the problem of Martin's *style:* a source of much affectionate amusement in Ottawa. While often giving the impression that he had great deeds in hand, he usually swamped both expectation and understanding in the morass of his rhetoric. As Peter C. Newman has written:

> In Parliament he sat hunched in his seat, holding himself with the tired pride of a man who daily meets Herculean claims on his resources, and was seldom reduced to the indignity of making a factual reply. Using a dozen vague, circumlocutory sentences where six short words would do, he spun out the smooth skein of Canada's foreign relations into webs of verbiage that he himself could not possibly have unravelled.[2]

This oratorical confusion was partly based on an honest devotion to the cause of Quiet Diplomacy: a conviction that peace initiatives could only work if they were kept as secret as possible. During Martin's time as External Affairs Minister (1963-1968), it was always difficult to know exactly what was happening about Vietnam — at least as far as Canada was concerned. But Martin was adept at hinting that *something* was under way: after the Americans resumed their air strikes on January 31, he announced that a cautious Canadian initiative, aimed at arranging a new Geneva conference, had drawn favourable reactions. Martin had already seen U Thant in New York and Dean Rusk in Washington; he let it be known that he was also planning meetings with the Indian and Polish Foreign Ministers to work out a joint ICC approach to the belligerents. Little more was heard of this plan, especially after the Poles were reported to be opposed to it. By that time, however, Martin had already taken a different tack: if an ICC approach was hopeless, then Ottawa would launch its own independent initiative, using the Canadian channel to Hanoi which Blair Seaborn had pursued so fruitlessly in 1964 and 1965.

This time there were two main differences. Instead of Seaborn, a senior diplomat but a man with no special standing in Asia, Martin would use Ronning, whom the North Vietnamese and the Chinese probably respected more than any other Canadian. This time, too, it would be a Canadian initiative; while Washington would be consulted, no one could ever accuse Ronning of being a mere messenger boy. There was even a convenient pretext for the mission since Pearson was among the heads of government who had received Ho Chi Minh's letter of January 24 and therefore Ronning could deliver his reply.

When Washington was told about the plan in late January, it reacted with almost comical distress. According to the analyst who compiled the Ronning chapter of the Pentagon Papers' diplomatic section, Ottawa's proposal "evoked formal US support and unvoiced US trepidations." The Americans regarded Ronning as an opponent of their Asian policies. Since he also hoped to visit Peking, Washington was convinced there was an "ulterior motive" behind his trip: a Canadian move to establish diplomatic relations with China and to bring it into the United Nations. But the Americans were still loudly proclaiming their desire for negotiations (even while planning to resume the bombing), and they could hardly risk a repetition of the La Pira fiasco. So they approved the Canadian initiative, while making quite clear that they had little hope for its success.

Ronning was in Washington on January 27; with Canadian Ambassador Charles Ritchie, he called on William Bundy at the State Department. Later that day Bundy sent a cable to Henry Cabot Lodge, who was again US Ambassador in Saigon:

> Canadian Ambassador Ritchie and former Canadian High Commissioner in New Delhi Ronning called on Bundy today and discussed planned visit by Amb. Ronning to Peking and Hanoi in near future. Ronning visit to be unofficial but he will travel with personal rank of

95

Ambassador and at request of Foreign Minister Martin. Ronning has long-standing invitation from Chicom Fonmin Chen Yi to visit CPR* extended when Ronning was Canadian Rep at 1962 Geneva Conference on Laos. Purpose of visit to sound out Peking and Hanoi on possible conference on Vietnam. Ronning said he without any illusions as to likelihood of success but thought visit in any event might be worthwhile.[3]

For the next few days there was heavy cable traffic between the State Department and the US Embassy in Ottawa where Ambassador Walton Butterworth was making frantic attempts to uncover Canadian motives for the Ronning mission. A large, ebullient career diplomat, Butterworth had easy access to both Martin and Pearson. As a young foreign service officer in the early 1930s, Butterworth had been posted to Ottawa where he and Pearson frequently played tennis together; three decades later he revived the former intimacy to the point where some of Pearson's cabinet colleagues thought that the American was taking awful liberties with the Prime Minister. In his cables to Washington, Butterworth would soon be suggesting that there was a definite difference of opinion between Pearson and Martin over the Ronning mission, with Pearson extremely sceptical. His comments on both men must be treated with caution since they represent an unconfirmed American view — Martin would later state that although the Ronning mission was his idea, Pearson had always supported it.[4] At any rate, the secret cables in both directions give a revealing picture of how Washington responded to the Canadian initiative with suspicions that verged on paranoia.

On January 28, Bundy cabled Butterworth: "It occurs to us that Ronning trip may well have ulterior motives in terms

* CPR — Chinese Peoples Republic

96

of Canadian feelers on Chicom representation in UN or even Canadian recognition." To this Butterworth replied:

> Ever since he became Minister of External Affairs two and a half years ago Martin has had the idea of using Chester Ronning, who was born in China and went to school with Chou En-lai, to help bring about recognition of the Chinese Communists by the UN or Canada or both. . . . Ronning is well-known in Canada as a Sinologist and has been more often than not critical of American Far Eastern policies.[5]

Butterworth kept digging away. He was soon telling Bundy that "incredible though it may seem", he had learned that Ronning's passport would read Special Emissary of Canadian Government with Personal Rank of Ambassador. After separate meetings with both Pearson and Martin, the American envoy reported on apparent differences between the two Canadians over the Ronning mission, as well as Martin's alleged political motives:

> Pearson confirmed Ronning mission was Martin's idea, that it entailed greater dangers than Martin had perhaps appreciated and that he had "scared the hell out of Paul about it last night"; . . . if anything went wrong, his government would disavow any involvement in the Ronning mission. . . .
> Martin volunteered that he had clearly in mind the domestic political scene and "Diefenbaker's insincere support of the US position in Vietnam" and that at some point he should demonstrate to the Canadian people that Canada had not just been a US satellite but had done what it could to bring about a solution.[6]

At the same time, Bundy was telling Lodge about Ronning's views on Asia and his long-standing links with China.

97

"Despite our private misgivings as to his personal views, we have naturally had to say we would have no objection to such visit and indeed could only welcome any constructive initiative."[7]

As the misgivings piled up in Washington, Dean Rusk entered the picture, sending a personal letter to Martin which touched on the American fears:

Dear Paul:

... I must, however, express a shade of concern at the information that we have just had from Walton Butterworth that Ronning's passport will apparently carry the appearance of a formal accreditation as your special emissary with the personal rank of Ambassador. . . .

I am also more seriously concerned at the possibility that Ronning may find himself engaged in discussion, especially in Peiping*, of the problems relating to Chinese representation at the UN and even, if I understood your last conversation with Walton Butterworth correctly, questions of recognition . . .

I think we shall both have a great deal of thinking to do on this subject in the months ahead and I hope that in the first instance we can do it on a very confidential basis between ourselves. I have therefore welcomed the indication that you are not discussing the Ronning trip with any other government, and I would end by repeating my hope and assumption that he will be listening only as to

---

* After their victory in 1949, the Chinese Communists established their government in Peking, which means "Northern Capital". Previously, the Chinese Nationalists had ruled the country from Nanking ("Southern Capital"), while referring to Peking as Peiping ("Northern Light"). Fervent American supporters of the Nationalists continued to use Peiping to bolster the illusion that Chiang Kai-shek and his followers on Taiwan were still the legal rulers of China.

any matters other than Vietnam, and that in any event we shall have a full opportunity to talk over with you whatever he picks up in any other area.

With warm regards, Sincerely, Dean Rusk.[8]

Concern was now spreading to some of Washington's key diplomatic missions, including the Consulate-General in Hong Kong, a large and sophisticated establishment where scores of American experts were engaged in the arcane discipline of China-watching. Ronning would pass through Hong Kong; in a cable to Rusk, Consul-General Edward E. Rice promised:

> We shall do what we can helpfully to influence Ronning's thinking if opportunity presents itself. Incidentally American in Hong Kong who will have fullest opportunity affect his thinking is NY Times correspondent Topping, who is his son-in-law.[9]*

From Saigon, Lodge was showing growing apprehension about the Ronning mission, complaining to Rusk that he wasn't fully aware of all the implications and that "once again we seem to be getting into direct contacts which affect the future of Vietnam and I do not know what to tell the Vietnamese." Rusk tried to reassure his ambassador in an "Eyes Only" cable which indicated Washington's total scepticism about the Canadian move:

---

* Seymour Topping at that time was based in Hong Kong as the *New York Times'* chief correspondent in Southeast Asia. Later an assistant managing editor of the newspaper, he told the author in 1973 that he was never asked by US officials to influence his father-in-law and that the Consul-General's suggestion was "another example of the utter naïveté of the State Department in its approach to Vietnam — a complete miscalculation of my character, Ronning's character, our relationship and my position as a newspaperman."

Following are my own personal comments about the Ronning visit to Hanoi:

Quite frankly, the Canadians themselves seem to be of divided minds about his trip. Ronning has not been helpful on Vietnam and I have no doubt strongly favours recognition of Peiping. Mike Pearson is definitely sceptical about the whole affair but was inclined to go along with Paul Martin's guarded approval for the trip.

I personally talked to Paul Martin about Ronning and emphasised that it was extremely important that Ronning do nothing to encourage a Hanoi miscalculation about our determination and do nothing to undermine the publicly stated position of the United States. Martin assured me that he would make that very clear to Ronning.

Actually, the Ronning trip was originally designed primarily for Peiping and I suspect that the question of recognition and Peiping membership in the UN was most on Ronning's mind. However, Peiping refused to let him come since Canada's attitude toward Vietnam made his visit "inopportune".

I can assure you there is no occult understanding between Washington and Ottawa on this matter. If you need to say anything to the South Vietnamese about the Ronning trip, you can tell them that he is on no mission for us, that he has been strongly advised not to say anything or do anything which would encourage Hanoi to believe that their effort will succeed and that his visit should be considered along with such efforts as have been made by many individuals to have a go at Hanoi. Quite frankly, I attach no importance to his trip and expect nothing out of it. . . .[10]

As Rusk stated, China had turned down Ronning's request for a visa, despite his long-standing invitation from Chen Yi. The Sino-Soviet dispute was then in full bloom, with the Chinese working to out-bid the Russians for the support of Communist and other "national liberation" movements in the Third World. For this reason, among others, Peking was taking a hard line on Vietnam, opposing any negotiations to end the war and openly advising the Vietnamese to keep on fighting until they achieved a total victory. Since the Chinese knew that Ronning was going to Hanoi in hopes of arranging negotiations, they would obviously want to dissociate themselves from his mission. But it is significant that Chen Yi, in a personal message to Ronning which left the door open for a future visit, said it was Canadian support for US actions in Vietnam which made a visit inopportune.[11] While Ottawa always maintained that Canada followed an independent line over Vietnam, this is not how it appeared to the Chinese.

But the North Vietnamese were quick to agree to a Ronning visit when they were approached in Hanoi by Victor Moore, Seaborn's successor on the ICC. Back in Saigon in early March, Moore told Lodge that Hanoi's acceptance was "immediate" and that the North Vietnamese seemed to be worried about the immense casualties which their army was encountering in the South — a view which must have encouraged Lodge in the belief that further escalation was the key to success.[12]

Whatever their motives, the North Vietnamese welcomed the Canadian envoy and eventually outlined a policy on negotiations which was significantly different from their standard position. For a few heady days it seemed just possible that Ottawa might pull off a diplomatic triumph which had eluded scores of other would-be peacemakers.

* * * * *

It started badly. When Ronning and Moore arrived in Hanoi on March 7, they were given separate escorts into the city. According to Ronning, the North Vietnamese were anxious that his visit should not be under ICC auspices since they were disillusioned with Canada's role on the Commission and regarded Canada as little more than an American satellite. Ronning was also told that there was no chance of a meeting with Ho Chi Minh, although Ho sent apologies, explaining that he was busy with political conferences.[13]

For the first few days Ronning was subjected to a strenuous round of talks with lesser leaders, including Foreign Minister Nguyen Duy Trinh. The 71-year-old envoy found these talks tiring and frustrating, with conversations wandering down blind alleys and always returning to the same intransigent dead end. He felt there was a team effort to wear him down, since long, hard hours of conversation with one group of officials would be followed, with little rest, by another session with a fresh team. Some talks were scheduled in the early morning, with scarcely 15 minutes notice, apparently to keep him off balance. Adding to the strain was the need to talk through interpreters, since Ronning spoke little French, although he used his Chinese with some officials.

Even worse, the North Vietnamese showed no signs of easing their position on negotiations. As they had with Seaborn, they told Ronning that they were winning the war, even though it would still be a long struggle which would probably lead to the Americans destroying Hanoi and the major port of Haiphong. Trinh and other officials repeatedly insisted that Washington must accept their Four Points as the basis for any negotiations; they were just as adamant on the role of the National Liberation Front as the sole representative of the people of South Vietnam. When the Canadian envoy argued that the Four Points were unworkable as a formula for talks, since they would amount to a total American surrender, he was told "that's the Americans' problem". Ronning also failed to convince his hosts that the Americans were different from the French and that it was a mistake to believe that they could be driven out by military means. In reply he was told that North Vietnam had few large industries, that small industries and government offices were being dispersed, that women and children were being evacuated from the capital and that the United States could never crush an agricultural society like North Vietnam.

It all seemed very unpromising. Then — near the end of his four-day visit — Ronning achieved a breakthrough during an interview with Prime Minister Pham Van Dong. At first Dong was just as obdurate as his colleagues had been, according to Ronning's report of the meeting which he presented to William Bundy in Washington in the following week:

> Towards the end of the interview, however, and under persistent questioning by Ronning about the conditions Hanoi would require to have met before entering into direct or indirect talks with the USA, the Prime Minister gave the following indication: North Vietnamese willingness to enter into some form of preliminary contact hinges on a commitment by the USA to cease "bombing and all acts of war against North Vietnam . . . unconditionally and for good".
>
> In reply to questioning he made it clear that this condition was limited to North Vietnamese territory and did not encompass US military activity in the South.
>
> It was not clear whether the commitment envisaged by Pham Van Dong was to be given publicly, or diplomatically (the translator used the term "declaration"). Furthermore, while Pham Van Dong conveyed the impression that Hanoi's response to such a move by the USA would lead to negotiating contacts, he gave no clarification of whether he envisaged these as being direct or indirect. He said: "In fact, our position includes many aspects. In brief, we can say that informal talks and a cessation of attacks against North Vietnam go together."

He did intimate, however, that he was soliciting a US response, and a further exchange with the USA through Canadian channels. "For our part," Pham Van Dong said, "we will look into the attitude of the USA, and with all understanding."

It was agreed that what had been said to Ronning would be conveyed to the USA as a Canadian understanding of the North Vietnamese position, and not on the basis of a request by North Vietnam to do so. It was also understood that Canada was not volunteering to act as a mediator.

Emphasis was laid on the importance of absolute secrecy in any exchange that might develop from Ronning's discussions. Earlier feelers had become public and the North Vietnamese had been forced to issue a denial.

Weary though he was, Ronning could see that Dong seemed to be making an important concession by agreeing to some form of talks or contacts in return for a halt to the bombing, instead of insisting that Washington should first accept the full Four Points (two of these points — a complete withdrawal of US troops and US recognition of the NLF — were unacceptable to the Americans). But Ronning was puzzled, asking Dong why Hanoi had not talked to the United States during the 37-day bombing pause. Somewhat cryptically, Dong replied that they had. Earlier the Soviet Ambassador had made the same point, telling Ronning that North Vietnam had responded to the pause, but refusing to disclose any details.

Despite this apparent breakthrough, Ronning returned from Hanoi in a gloomy mood, according to American reports. To Rice in Hong Kong, he described the results of his mission by quoting an old Chinese saying — that he had "travelled ten thousands miles to present a feather" — and added that he was more pessimistic about the long-range

Vietnamese problem than he had been before the trip. To Bundy in Washington, he "expressed his personal opinion that the offer of talks for a complete halt to the bombing was separate from the '4 points' but added that, on balance, he frankly did not himself think anything significant had emerged from his visit."

These were American assessments of Ronning's attitude. They were almost certainly coloured by Washington's strong resistance to any negotiations at that time. Ronning's own recollection is significantly different. Seven years later he said that Hanoi had made a very important concession by agreeing to talks in return for a bombing halt and that both Pearson and Martin were excited by his report. If Ronning was pessimistic, it was only because he knew how the Americans would react.[14]

Ronning was right. For the next two months Ottawa and Washington engaged in a polite but persistent diplomatic struggle, with the Canadians pressing for some response to Hanoi's overture, and the Americans again scrambling to avoid committing themselves to negotiations on any terms that North Vietnam might possibly accept.

From the start the Americans were openly suspicious of Hanoi's apparent concession. At their Washington meeting, Bundy told Ronning that the North Vietnamese "ploy" was clever, since the bombing question had always been linked in the past with acceptance of the Four Points. Therefore, he added, if Washington now accepted Hanoi's offer, it would also be implicitly accepting the Four Points.

Such sophistry hardly indicates a burning desire to reach negotiations: it is not surprising that Ottawa heard nothing more on the subject for several weeks. For Martin this was an especially frustrating period. Through his own efforts the Canadian channel to Hanoi was again in operation and the North Vietnamese had used it to convey a concession which Martin regarded as significant.[15] There might now be at least

105

some faint hope of negotiations, but the Americans were refusing even to reply and this would certainly damage Canada's credibility in Hanoi.

Finally, at 9:05 am on April 22, Martin's impatience boiled over and he placed a phone call to Bundy. Martin said he was concerned at the long interval since Ronning's visit and implied he had heard that Hanoi was also concerned. It was important to establish with Hanoi that Canada was really trying to foster peace. He felt very strongly that the Canadians had to go back to the North Vietnamese with something — even nothing — even something contrived.

Bundy replied that there was no question of contriving a response. He was, in fact, working on a message to Ottawa, but the State Department did not feel it would be propitious to move "while things are at white heat".[16] However, the conversation did stir Bundy into action. On the same day he sent a memo to Rusk:

> Paul Martin is very anxious for a prompt response on the Ronning mission. We still do not see much in it but plainly our relations with Paul Martin alone would dictate as forthcoming a response as we can make. I have drafted a reply. . . .[17]

Four days later, and more than six weeks after Ronning had left Hanoi, Washington finally delivered a memorandum to Ottawa which agreed that the Canadian channel should be kept open, but said that the US had refrained from making any reply because of the political crisis in Saigon (where the government was still reeling from strikes and demonstrations in several leading cities). The Americans were still suspicious of Dong's offer of talks in return for a permanent cessation of the bombing, since this was probably intended to be linked with US acceptance of the Four Points — "although a contrary interpretation is conceivable."

106

At any rate, Ronning could tell the North Vietnamese that Washington was ready for discussions or negotiations "without any preconditions whatsoever". It was also ready to discuss a halt to the bombing in return for reciprocal measures by Hanoi. But it would not stop bombing "as a unilateral and non-reciprocal precondition to the holding of discussions."[18]

Now it was up to Ottawa to find out whether North Vietnam would welcome Ronning for a second time. On May 21, Major Jerry Donahue, a Canadian officer with the ICC in Hanoi, reported to Moore in Saigon on a meeting with Col. Ha Van Lau. Donahue was given an *aide memoire* which criticised a speech in Toronto by Pearson, in which he had proposed an immediate ceasefire followed by a phased withdrawal of North Vietnamese and American troops from South Vietnam under ICC auspices. The United States had been quick to endorse the proposal; it had been attacked by the Chinese as "an old American trick, not worthy of comment." Although Pearson later denied that his proposal had originated in Washington, it had also annoyed Hanoi:

It is to be regretted that this proposal conforms neither to the fundamental provisions of the 1954 Geneva Agreements on Vietnam, nor to the actual situation in Vietnam. It makes no distinction between the USA which is the aggressor and the Vietnamese people who are the victims of aggression fighting in self-defense. It does not meet the four-point stand of the DRVN Govt. However, out of good will, we consider that Mr Ronning's visit to Hanoi may be agreed to as proposal by the CND Govt. The timing of the visit will be intimated in due course.[19]

So the door to Hanoi was still open, if only by a narrow crack. As Ronning prepared to leave, however, Ottawa became concerned about apparent US attempts to undermine his mission in advance. In Saigon, Moore called on Lodge to report that he had found a "will to talk" on his latest trip to Hanoi. But Moore stressed the danger of leaks and too much publicity about peace feelers, stating that Hanoi had "played ball" by keeping quiet on the first Ronning mission and he thought they would do so again. In particular, he deplored a statement by a State Department spokesman on June 3 which "gave in public almost exactly what the substance was of what the Canadians were planning to say in private." From Ottawa, Butterworth also reported on Canadian concern over Washington newspaper stories which said that the United States had sent a new message to Hanoi, pledging its willingness to stop bombing the North if Hanoi stopped infiltrating troops into the South.[20]

The Canadians would have been even more concerned if they had known about secret Washington plans to launch a major extension of the air war against North Vietnam. After months of pressure from the Joint Chiefs of Staff, President Johnson had approved strikes against the petroleum, oil and lubricant supplies and depots in the North. The Joint Chiefs predicted that these so-called POL strikes would bring Hanoi to the conference table or else cause the insurgency to wither away, although the Central Intelligence Agency warned that they wouldn't cripple the Communists' military operations.[21]

Plans for the POL strikes were being completed at the Pentagon at the same time as the State Department was preparing its message for Ronning to take to Hanoi. At the last moment it finally dawned on the Administration that the raids would sabotage the Ronning mission and have serious diplomatic and political repercussions. Rusk, who was in Europe, sent an urgent top-secret cable to McNamara:

> I am deeply disturbed by general international revulsion, and perhaps a great deal at home, if it becomes known that we took an action which sabotaged the Ronning

mission to which we had given our agreement. I recognise agony of this problem for all concerned. We could make arrangements to get an immediate report from Ronning. If he has a negative report, as we expect, that provides a firmer base for the action we contemplate and would make a difference to people like (British Prime Minister) Wilson and Pearson. If, on the other hand, he learns that there is any serious breakthrough toward peace, the President would surely want to know of that before an action which would knock such a possibility off the tracks. I strongly recommend therefore against ninth or tenth (of June). I regret this because of my maximum desire to support you and your colleagues in your tough job.[22]

Rusk had sent a similar message to the President, who agreed to postpone the strikes. As Rusk's cable indicates, Washington was already convinced that the second Ronning mission would be a failure. Although Ottawa didn't know it at the time, the Americans were only waiting for Ronning's return in order to launch yet another major escalation of the conflict.

* * * * *

These were difficult days for Paul Martin. After Ronning's first mission in May, his initial optimism had been cooled by Washington's sceptical and tardy response. Looking back in later years, Martin would date his disillusionment with American policies from this point. When he had threatened to send Ronning back to Hanoi to report to the North Vietnamese that there was no US reply to their offer, the Americans had finally sent a memorandum which Martin regarded as meaningless. With the American refusal to accept Pham Van Dong's concession as a serious move toward peace, Martin started to believe that they were not really interested in negotiations, but were determined to win a military victory.[23]

None of this was apparent at the time, since Martin believed that to differ openly with Washington would demolish any lingering chances for a successful Canadian initiative. Judging by his public actions — and his private communications to Washington — he was still clinging to the faint hope that Canada could succeed where all other peacemakers had so far failed.

Yet Martin knew only too well that if the Canadian initiative received too much publicity, the North Vietnamese would reject it. While publicity might be gratifying in terms of domestic politics, it could only be diplomatically disastrous. When Ronning's first mission was reported in the press, Martin had refrained from giving any indication of his hopes for a breakthrough to negotiations. With Ronning back in Hanoi from June 14 to 17, Martin confirmed the fact of the mission, but again refused to give details. At the same time, Ronning was under strict instructions to say nothing to anyone about his mission until he had reported back to Ottawa. Several cables in the diplomatic section of the Pentagon Papers show that the Americans tried but failed to get information out of Ronning when he came back through the Laotian capital of Vientiane; from Saigon, Lodge told Rusk somewhat testily that Moore was also refusing to talk.

If Martin was worried about leaks from the American side, he was just as concerned about Washington's military plans. In fact he had a shrewd premonition that some major move was imminent. On June 20, the US Embassy in Ottawa told Washington that Martin had expressed "grave concern that any escalation in military action in Vietnam by US in immediate future would jeopardize Canadian good faith with Hanoi and make it appear US used Ronning as means of obtaining negative readout on negotiations which would justify escalation."[24] This, of course, was exactly what Rusk had intimated in his cable to McNamara.

With the Canadians keeping such close secrecy, the Americans had to come to Ottawa to discover the results of Ronning's second mission. Bundy and other State Department officials flew to Ottawa on June 21 for a lengthy meeting with Martin, Ronning and other senior Canadians. The American reports of this meeting make clear that Martin was right in his fears that premature publicity and continuing escalation had helped to undermine the Canadian initiative.[25]

Ronning told the Americans that Foreign Minister Nguyen Duy Trinh was the highest official whom he saw (he was told that Pham Van Dong was out of the capital). Trinh said he was disappointed with the US oral message which was similar to what he had already read in the newspapers. He also charged that the US had been escalating the war since Ronning's first visit in March. Scorning the US offer, Trinh flatly rejected any suggestion that Hanoi should pay a price for a bombing halt. When pressed by Ronning, the Foreign Minister said that North Vietnam was sticking to its March proposal that talks could follow an end to the bombing. The US would also have to "recognise the NLF position", abide by the terms of the Geneva Agreements and withdraw its forces and bases from South Vietnam. When he was pressed further, however, Trinh stated specifically that acceptance of the Four Points and a cessation of fighting in South Vietnam were *not* preconditions for preliminary talks between North Vietnam and the United States.

These were crucial points and Martin was anxious that the Americans should grasp them. Prompted by Martin, Ronning said he was absolutely convinced that Hanoi was ready to talk solely on the basis of an end to the bombing, although he thought that the North Vietnamese wanted informal discussions, rather than formal negotiations or a Geneva-type conference.

Bundy was unimpressed. Reporting to Rusk on the same day, he said that the result of Ronning's trip was clearly

111

negative and that he (Bundy) remained convinced that the Four Points would still be in the picture if the preliminary talks led to substantive negotiations. The Americans also took comfort from Ronning's attitude, which they found much more sober and subdued than it had been after his March trip.

By this point the Americans were treating the Canadian initiative with thinly veiled contempt — especially since they had little interest in negotiations and were impatient to launch their delayed attacks on the POL sites. At the same time the Canadians were fast losing any credibility they retained at the other end of their channel. Trinh accused Canada of joining the US in another "peace offensive" and wondered how it was possible for Ronning to be in Hanoi while the war was being escalated. He also complained that Ronning's presentation had shown a lack of appreciation of Hanoi's position. There were only a few crumbs of comfort: Trinh said that North Vietnam wanted to keep the Canadian channel open for any further developments; on his final day in Hanoi, Ronning was told by a lesser official that North Vietnam still had confidence in Canadian sincerity and good will.

In the presence of Bundy and the other Americans, Martin seized eagerly on these few crumbs, repeatedly emphasising that Hanoi wanted to keep the channel open. When the talks continued over dinner, Martin complained that the American position had not been forthcoming enough and that premature publicity from Washington might have queered the Canadian mission. By the end of the evening, Bundy felt confident that Martin would not repeat these recriminations in public; he also reported that Martin had agreed Washington could not have accepted Hanoi's offer of talks for a bombing halt.

Seven years later, Martin strongly denied that he had ever agreed with Bundy on the bombing.[26] Even at the time it was

112

evident to the Americans that Ottawa would still persist in its tiresome efforts to promote a peace that Washington had no intention of accepting. When the State Department reported on the dinner meeting to Lodge in Saigon, it noted that "Ronning seemed more responsive to our approach than we had seen him before but Martin clearly remains determined to find some role for Canada in peace-making efforts in future."[27]

But the Americans told the Canadians that they saw no immediate prospects for a further peace initiative. Bundy maintained that the American military pressure in the South, and the American bombing of the North, were having an effect on Hanoi. If the political situation in Saigon could be stabilised, Hanoi might start to show some signs of "give" in three or four months, although Bundy was not hopeful that North Vietnam would be ready to call off its support for the war in the South by the end of the year.

This was the standard American position. There could be no question of negotiations until the Saigon government was strong enough to stand the shock. At the same time, Washington would continue to punish North Vietnam until its leaders were forced to accept negotiations on US terms. These fatal and foolish assumptions were based on a blind faith in American military might and technological skill; they consistently overlooked the human factor — especially North Vietnam's stubborn will to resist. Like Seaborn two years earlier, Ronning told the Americans that the North Vietnamese expected that the US would eventually bomb Hanoi and Haiphong and lay waste most of North Vietnam, although they were still confident of eventual victory.

None of this made the slightest impression on Bundy, a cool, introverted intellectual and ex-CIA official who was one of the foremost hawks in the Administration and one of the few who was kept informed of virtually every military or diplomatic action that was either planned or underway. When he came to Ottawa, Bundy must have known that the POL strikes had been postponed, pending Ronning's return from Hanoi, and that his negative report would lead to their speedy implementation. It is not surprising that Bundy failed to mention these plans to the Canadians. But according to the State Department account of the dinner meeting, Bundy went much further along the path of deliberate deception:

> Mr Bundy specifically said that we had no intention of bombing the cities of Hanoi and Haiphong, or mining the Haiphong harbour. Ronning had given an interesting account of the air raid shelters being constructed in Hanoi, and Mr Bundy said flatly that they would not need these shelters. Ronning also expressed grave concern over any US action that tended to throw the North Vietnamese into the arms of the Chicoms, which he thought would be disastrous, both in stiffening the North Vietnamese position and in bringing about heavy Chicom influence and eventual control in North Vietnam. Mr Bundy said that we saw the same danger, and that it was a major element in our not contemplating the mining of Haiphong.
>
> During the above discussions, Mr Bundy twice made clear that we might well consider actions within our present policy and within the above analysis of Chicom reactions. These references were not picked up by the Canadians, but can hardly have gone unnoticed.

As Bundy must have known, the POL targets included tank farms and other large storage sites on the outskirts of Hanoi and Haiphong. Clearly Bundy was determined to befuddle the Canadians, while covering himself against future recriminations by hinting that some sort of military action was contemplated "within our present policy". Despite evidence that the Americans frequently bombed civilian targets and caused civilian casualties in the North, Washington maintained that it only attacked military targets. It was later argued that the POL strikes were not directed against the civilian centres in Hanoi and Haiphong — this was the apparent basis of Bundy's sophistry. There are times, however, when sophistry and diplomatic evasion are nothing more than outright lying.

On June 22, the day after the Ottawa meetings, Washington authorised raids on the POL targets in the Hanoi-Haiphong area. The strikes were delayed by bad weather, but on June 29 wave after wave of American planes struck the storage depots. A report from the Seventh Air Force called the operation "the most significant, the most important strike of the war". According to the Pentagon Papers, "official Washington reacted with mild jubilation to the reported success of the POL strikes and took satisfaction in the relatively mild reaction of the international community to the escalation." Once again, however, American optimism and American military estimates proved unfounded. By August the flow of men and supplies from North Vietnam to the South was continuing at its former level and "it was clear that the POL strikes had been a failure."[28]

Despite their lack of success, the POL strikes marked the first time that American planes had bombed Hanoi. Although Martin and Ronning refrained at the time from making public how Bundy had deceived them, there was anger and bitterness in Ottawa. It would now be quite clear to the North Vietnamese that the Ronning missions *were* part of Washington's fraudulent peace offensive and that the Canadian envoy had been used to justify a major extension of the war. Adding to Canada's distress, US Undersecretary of State George Ball told a television interviewer on July 1 that "there was nothing in what Ambassador Ronning brought back which gave any encouragement that Hanoi was prepared to come to the conference table."

This was another hard slap in the face for Canada. When pressed by Diefenbaker in the House of Commons, Martin

115

had only said that "it would be wrong at this stage to assess the results of the Ronning visit in one way or another." Now the Americans had deliberately disregarded all the Canadian pleas that contacts with Hanoi could only be maintained if strict secrecy was kept. Ball was not only guilty of breaching diplomatic confidence — he was also making sure that the North Vietnamese would no longer have any faith in Canadian good will or in Canada as an intermediary. Just two years after Blair Seaborn made his first trip to Hanoi, the Canadian channel was consigned to the diplomatic junk yard.

* * * * *

By now the Americans were relentlessly punishing an enemy that refused to capitulate. As the bombs rained down on Hanoi and Haiphong, Washington announced that its troop strength in South Vietnam would be increased to 375,000 by the end of 1966 and to 425,000 by the spring of 1967 (it was eventually to pass the half-million mark). Despite a rash of peace proposals from various world leaders, there was no sign of any change in the diplomatic deadlock. The North Vietnamese still refused to negotiate while the bombing continued; Johnson said the bombs would fall until Hanoi reduced its military activity in the South.

By late 1966 the prospects for peace looked even dimmer than they had during the previous winter, when Martin launched the first Ronning mission. By then, too, Ottawa had learned that the Americans were not to be trusted; the Canadians also realised that their standing in Hanoi had been severely compromised. But Martin refused to call it quits, apparently still hoping for a diplomatic success that had eluded U Thant, Pope Paul, President Charles de Gaulle, Prime Minister Indira Gandhi and a host of lesser luminaries whose overtures had all been rejected by either Hanoi or Washington. This time Martin conducted his own probe, travelling to Warsaw in early November for talks with Adam Rapacki, his Polish counterpart, only to discover that the two old antagonists on the ICC still had sharply different positions on the war. Moving on to Moscow, Martin urged Andrei Gromyko, the Soviet Foreign Minister, to have the Soviet Union authorise new responsibilities for the ICC as an initial step toward peace. But this probe also fizzled out, with Martin admitting that the Russians had reacted coolly to his suggestion, and the Chinese taking advantage of his visit to assail Moscow for engaging in a "peace talk fraud".

Although Martin didn't know it at the time, something *was* in the wind and it even involved the Poles who were giving him such dusty answers. This was the project which the Americans had code-named Marigold. It started on the day that the POL strikes were launched and was the initiative of Janusz Lewandowski, a 35-year-old Polish diplomat who was his country's chief delegate on the ICC in Vietnam. At top-secret meetings with Lodge in Saigon and North Vietnamese leaders in Hanoi, the Pole patiently worked out a formula for peace talks which seemed to be acceptable to both sides. Although the Americans were dubious, there were signs that the North Vietnamese would talk about a political settlement without first insisting on a bombing halt. In early December plans were almost completed for a meeting between the two sides in Warsaw when the Americans resumed bombing Hanoi after a two-week pause caused by bad weather. Despite urgent warnings from the Poles, there were more heavy raids on Hanoi in mid-December. That was the end of Marigold. The Poles told the Americans that the North Vietnamese were no longer interested in talks.[29]

When news of Marigold was leaked to the press in the following month, the Poles were quick to charge that the North Vietnamese had been ready and eager to talk, but the Americans had deliberately sabotaged the plan. This was a predictable reaction: the truth was certainly more complex although it could hardly reassure those — like Martin — who retained some faith in Washington's desire for negotiations. After the failure of his peace offensive in the previous winter, President Johnson remained convinced that more military pressure was the only prescription for Hanoi. This meant that the balance of forces in the Administration was still heavily in favour of escalation, rather than negotiation. On the basis of his direct experience of Marigold and other peace probes, Chester Cooper concluded that there was never any deliberate attempt to sabotage the diplomatic moves but that "the Administration, as of late 1966 and early 1967, was just not interested in negotiations to the extent necessary to prevent military actions from interfering with or even negating diplomatic initiatives."[30]

This was certainly the case with Canada's last major effort to bring peace to Vietnam which also collapsed amid more American bombing. Despite his rebuffs in Warsaw and Moscow, Martin had not given up the struggle. In April he unveiled a four-point plan as a preliminary to discussions. The plan involved a progressive reapplication of the Geneva ceasefire terms: (1) restoration of the Demilitarized Zone between North and South Vietnam and a halt to the bombing of the North; (2) military activity and strengths in the South to be held at their existing levels; (3) a cessation of all hostilities; (4) repatriation of prisoners and a withdrawal of outside forces and a dismantling of military bases in the South.

It was a measure of Martin's desperation that he made his proposal *publicly* — for him a most uncharacteristic step. But as he told MPs, it was worth exploring new directions since the diplomatic impasse had reached a point where, for the first time in 16 months, no new initiatives, either public or private, appeared within sight. Martin also said he was not optimistic that his plan would be acceptable to both sides. Hanoi quickly proved him right, rejecting it as "a crafty scheme of the US imperialists . . . which does not make a

118

clear distinction between the aggressor and those who oppose aggression."

But the Americans saw Martin's proposal as a windfall and were quick to adapt it to suit their own military and diplomatic requirements. As Ottawa must have known, the plan had a special appeal to the United States since American troops in the northern part of South Vietnam had been taking heavy casualties from North Vietnamese forces operating in the northern section of the DMZ. One week after Martin's statement, the State Department went a step further, proposing that both sides withdraw their forces to 10 miles beyond the DMZ and then consider talks leading to a further de-escalation. Immediately after the public announcement, Averell Harriman told the Soviet Embassy that the US regarded the plan as an important first step toward a settlement. At the same time, Washington asked Ottawa to approach the Indians and the Poles about the possibility of an ICC force in an expanded DMZ.

Since the revised proposal was obviously to the advantage of the Americans, it was always likely to be rejected by Hanoi. But rejection was made certain when bombers struck major new targets in Haiphong on the *same evening* as Washington's announcement. Learning about the planned raids at the last moment, horrified officials at the State Department had urged their cancellation, but no one had the power to reverse the order, or the courage to approach the President. After the raids the Russians told the Americans that they could no longer regard their DMZ proposal as a serious move to peace. Within another day Hanoi had rejected the US plan as a "trick".[31]

Once again a Canadian peace initiative had been perverted by Washington's relentless drive for military victory. Once again Canada was made to appear as nothing more than an American accomplice in the steady extension of the conflict. Yet in the following month Martin could still assure the

119

House of Commons that "if we do have a credibility in Hanoi it is because it is thought that as a friend of the United States we rightfully enjoy the confidence of the United States."

The North Vietnamese must have read Martin's statement with disdainful shrugs. By that time they had few illusions about Canadian "good will". As early as the previous January the North Vietnamese official newspaper Nhan Dan had stated in a commentary on Canadian arms sales to the United States:

> The Canadian government's action proves that statements to the effect that Canada takes a "neutral" attitude towards the Vietnamese problem and attaches a great importance to the search for a solution for putting an end to the war are false. . . . The Vietnamese people know that the Canadian government has always supported and tolerated the intensification of the armed aggression of the United States.[32]

* * * * *

By now there were many Canadians who would have regarded Hanoi's accusation as very close to the literal truth. As the bombs rained down on North Vietnam and television screens were filled with pictures of the ghastly carnage in the South, there was growing opposition within Canada to Ottawa's complicity in the American war. This opposition was especially strong among university professors and students; increasingly it came to focus on Canada's contribution to the American war machine under the terms of the Defence Production Sharing Agreement.

Dating from 1959, the DPSA had been requested by Ottawa as a means of keeping the Canadian armed forces equipped with modern weapons without disastrous effects to the Canadian balance of payments. It established that American purchases of military equipment in Canada would be

120

kept roughly equivalent to Canadian military purchases in the United States. This meant that a wide range of Canadian firms was soon deeply involved in filling sub-contracts from the US defence industry.

By 1966 Canada was selling more than $300-million of military materials to the United States a year. Inevitably a great deal of this equipment found its way to Vietnam. Canadian cabinet ministers behaved like a gaggle of Pontius Pilates — disclaiming any responsibility for the way in which the material was used once it passed into American hands. Their complacency was only slightly shaken when Canadian journalists began to compile lists which showed the extent to which Canadian products were involved in the taking of Vietnamese lives and the destruction of the Vietnamese countryside.

As they dropped their bombs on North Vietnamese towns or seared Southern villages with their rockets and napalm, American planes were often guided by Canadian-made Marconi Doppler Navigation Systems and used bombing computers built in Rexdale, Ontario. The bombs could have been armed with dynamite shipped from Valleyfield, Quebec; polystyrene, a major component in the napalm, was supplied by Dow Chemical. Defoliants came from Naugatuck Chemicals in Elmira, Ontario, and air-to-ground rockets were furnished by the Ingersoll Machine and Tool Company. On the ground, American infantry and artillery units were supplied by De Havilland Caribou built at Malton, Ontario. Less lethal Canadian products included Bata boots for the troops and the famous green berets of the Special Forces which came from Dorothea Knitting Mills in Toronto. Nor were all the profits left to private industry: Canadian Arsenals Ltd., a Crown Corporation, sold small arms, fill for artillery shells, mines, bombs, grenades, torpedo warheads, depth charges and rockets. Canadian government salesmen drummed up business around the United States and distributed their

121

annual catalogue, Canadian Defence Commodities, which Walter Stewart aptly described as a kind of Warmonger's Shopping Guide.[33]

It was always hypocritical for Canadian ministers to deny responsibility for the ultimate use of these weapons, components and other war materials. Article 17 of the 1954 Geneva Agreements specifically prohibited the importing of arms into Vietnam. As a member of the ICC, Canada was pledged to enforce that convention. By feeding the American war machine, the Canadian government mocked its obligations and demolished its pretensions to be playing an objective and impartial role in Vietnam. Rarely have gamekeepers turned poachers with such a vengeance.

Hard-nosed defenders of the DPSA were quick to point out that the military sales were vital to Canadian prosperity. In 1966 Ottawa estimated that Canadian exports under the agreement provided full-time employment for 13,000 to 15,000 Canadians and affected another 110,000 in varying degrees. Nor were the Canadian products vital to US requirements, since Washington never spent more than one per cent of its military budget in Canada and could easily have found alternative sources of supply within its borders. It would be much more serious, however, if the Americans were deprived of Canadian raw materials, rather than finished products or manufactured components. Canadian nickel, aluminum, iron ore and steel *were* essential to the US war machine; it was no coincidence that these exports rose dramatically during the height of the Vietnam conflict in the 1960s.[34]

But it was the bombs, the dynamite and the other weaponry which captured public attention and caused large numbers of Canadians to feel revulsion at their government's Vietnam policies and to question Ottawa's claims to be both peacekeeper and peacemaker. Some of the tougher-minded members of the cabinet were always prepared to ignore the cries from the campus ("How many votes has Jim Eayrs?"

122

might have been their motto). But Pearson was proud of his own university background and his generally high standing with the academic community; throughout his time in office he strove to keep in touch with the professors and was always sensitive to their demands for a more independent Canadian foreign policy. In early 1967 he showed particular sensitivity to a letter from nearly 400 University of Toronto professors, including the Faculty Committee on Vietnam at his own Victoria College, which called upon Ottawa to reveal all military production contracts related in any way to Vietnam and to consider refusing to sell arms to the United States until its intervention in the war was ended.

In a formal reply to the professors in March, Pearson defended the economic necessity of the DPSA, including its contribution to Canadian industrial research and the development of Canadian technology. He also argued that it would be impossible for Ottawa to ascertain the present whereabouts of all the military items purchased by the Americans: "Such equipment goes into the general inventory of the US armed forces and may be used for such purposes and in such parts of the world as the US government may see fit."

Pearson's statement was even more revealing when it underlined the extent to which successive Canadian governments had hobbled Canadian foreign policy by actively seeking to enmesh Canada in the American industrial and military complex. He traced the DPSA back to the Hyde Park Declaration of 1941 which laid the basis for co-operation in World War Two, especially in defence production. He described this co-operation as necessary and logical to meet the postwar demands of collective security. It seemed obvious to Pearson that there was no way Canada could start dismantling this political and military structure:

> . . . it is clear that the imposition of an embargo on the export of military equipment to the USA, and con-

comitant termination of the Production Sharing Agreements, would have far-reaching consequences which no Canadian government could contemplate with equanimity. It would be interpreted as a notice of withdrawal on our part from continental defence and even from the collective arrangements of the Atlantic Alliance.

In other words, Canada had to supply military equipment to the Americans in Vietnam because Canada was an ally of the United States in the defence of Western Europe and North America. Rarely has a Canadian leader made such an abject admission of Canada's lack of independence in foreign affairs. As Kenneth McNaught responded:

No more concise or authoritative statement has been made on the subject. After his letter no one can maintain that acceptance of continental integration in defense production and planning leaves us free in general foreign policy — leaves us free to accept one part of the American alliance structure while rejecting other parts of it. Nor can anyone seriously doubt that it is this integration that has produced, as James Eayrs has put it, the smooth Canadians who haunt the corridors of Washington with their confidential, ineffective briefs.[35]

The professors were far from the only Canadians who were aghast at Ottawa's bland acceptance of its impotence over Vietnam. Within the government, Privy Council President Walter Gordon — already known as a staunch nationalist — had become alarmed by the level of violence in the war. Gordon knew that he could make no impact by raising the issue in cabinet, where Martin had always managed to block any serious discussion on Vietnam. So he decided to breach the principle of cabinet solidarity and speak out publicly.

124

In a speech delivered in Toronto on May 13, Gordon stressed the dangers and the futility of the American military policy, stating that Washington had become entangled in a bloody civil war which could not be justified on either moral or strategic grounds. He was careful not to sound merely anti-American, since he built his powerful indictment on statements by American opponents of the war. Specifically he endorsed their call for a suspension of the bombing, a halt to the US military offensive in the South and an American statement of willingness to negotiate directly with the NLF. As Denis Smith has noted:

> These appeals amounted to much more than the Canadian government had ever called for in public; and Gordon concluded with a conspicuous nudge at his cabinet colleagues:
> "I hope Canadians in all walks of life and in all political parties — including especially Mr. Pearson and Mr. Martin — will continue to do everything in their power to press the Americans to stop the bombing. If we fail to do this, we must be prepared to share the responsibility of those whose policies involve the gravest risks for all mankind."[36]

There was uproar in Ottawa over this blatant dissent from the hallowed principles of Quiet Diplomacy. Within hours Martin was calling for Gordon's resignation. At a special cabinet meeting, a tired and angry Pearson delivered a statement which was designed to heal the breach. Although Pearson was implicitly critical of his old friend and political ally, Gordon felt that he could live with the statement because it requested the United States — "as the strongest of the warring parties" — to end the bombing and start negotiations.

In return for this statement Gordon promised to refrain from making any public comment on the incident. He was soon to feel betrayed when Pearson then delivered an even sharper rebuke in the Liberal caucus and went out to tell reporters that Gordon had been "criticised and disciplined". But there was some consolation in the fact that he received nearly 1,000 letters in response to his speech — an extremely high total for any Canadian politician on any subject — and nearly all of them were favourable. His speech had come close to the position of the NDP and the various anti-war groups in Canada; it was evident that he — and they — were speaking for large numbers of Canadians.

None of this public unrest caused the government to become significantly more outspoken on the war. Ottawa was determined to remain faithful to the doctrine which Pearson had affirmed in his letter to the Toronto professors, stating that "confidential and quiet arguments by a responsible government are usually more effective than public ones."

Yet quiet arguments were *never* effective with the Americans over Vietnam. In June, Martin took Gordon with him to the NATO Council meeting in Luxembourg. As though determined to show Gordon what Quiet Diplomacy was all about, he arranged a special private session on Vietnam, during which he was highly critical of US policy on the war. Gordon was surprised and impressed by Martin's frankness; he was equally impressed that none of the other foreign ministers backed the Canadian case and that Dean Rusk coldly rejected all of Martin's arguments in a shallow and supercilious reply.[37]

By this point even Martin was losing hope of influencing the Americans through private persuasion. With the failure of the Ronning missions in the previous year, he had started to suspect that the Americans were more interested in military victory than serious negotiations. Now he decided it was time for some public prodding, choosing for his platform the United Nations — the scene of so many successful Canadian diplomatic initiatives and the repository of Pearson and Martin's hopes for a more peaceful world.

126

Discussing Vietnam in a speech to the General Assembly on September 27, Martin notably refrained from using any of the Cold War rhetoric with which he had formerly supported American views on the origins and nature of the war. Even more significantly, he openly called upon the Americans to stop bombing the North as a necessary first step toward negotiations. According to Martin, he spoke out because it was evident that private diplomacy had been totally unsuccessful and because there were no new diplomatic initiatives underway.[38] His call for a bombing halt was stronger than Pearson's diffident suggestion of a bombing pause in his Temple Speech of April 1965. But it came at a time when the Americans had been devastating the North for over two years and after more than a decade of Canadian support for Washington's brutal and disastrous intervention in the affairs of Vietnam. It was a bit late in the day to start seeing the light.

* * * * *

There were no more Canadian initiatives for peace in Vietnam. When Washington and Hanoi finally agreed to negotiate in the spring of 1968, it was not through the efforts of helpful intermediaries or the use of secret channels. Instead it was caused by a combination of military and political events, including the Tet Offensive (which both sides claimed as a victory) and mounting resistance within the United States to the Administration's war. When Senator Eugene McCarthy won 40 per cent of the vote in New Hampshire's Presidential primary, and Senator Robert Kennedy announced he would also seek the Democratic nomination, the war became a dangerously divisive issue. On March 31, Johnson took the decisive step, announcing that he had ordered a halt to all air and naval bombardment of North Vietnam above the 20th parallel and that he would not stand for re-election. Within three days Hanoi had given a positive response; within a

127

month both sides had agreed to hold preliminary talks in Paris. Negotiations would prove prolonged and difficult, and it would be more than four years before the Paris Agreement led to the withdrawal of American troops from South Vietnam, although not to an end of the fighting among the Vietnamese themselves.

It is noteworthy that the breakthrough occurred when Johnson went more than halfway to meeting Pham Van Dong's proposal to Ronning of March 1966. By stopping the bombing north of the 20th parallel, he was releasing about 90 per cent of North Vietnam's population from the terror of the American strikes. On November 1, Johnson went the rest of the way — stopping *all* air, naval and artillery bombardment of the North — and making it possible for the preliminary talks in Paris to develop into formal negotiations among the Americans, the South Vietnamese, the North Vietnamese and the National Liberation Front. After two more years of further escalation, Washington had been forced to meet Hanoi's terms by halting the bombing while the ground war continued unabated in the South.

So it can be argued that Ronning had the key to negotiations in 1966 and that the war was only prolonged by Washington's stubborn belief that greater military pressure would force Hanoi to modify its terms. While there is much truth in that view, it is also over-simplified. Although the Americans were undoubtedly grudging, evasive and deceitful in their response to peace probes by Canada and other third parties, the North Vietnamese were equally difficult. From 1964 through 1967, the North was quick to denounce every American offer of negotiations as a swindle or a hoax. Often Hanoi had good reason, but not *all* the American offers were based upon a demand for their capitulation or sabotaged by further escalation: some at least might have been profitably explored. There were, in fact, many tentative peace feelers from Hanoi, including the one to Ronning. But the

Americans had cause for suspicion since time and time again, they received signals and messages through various channels which were either subsequently denied by Hanoi or else contradicted by signals and messages conveyed by other sources. In such an atmosphere of mutual distrust, neither side felt secure in making the first definitive, unmistakable move toward peace until Johnson's offer of March 1968.[39]

It is also a mistake to see these events exclusively through Canadian eyes, since this can place undue importance on the Seaborn and Ronning missions. As Washington saw them, the Canadian initiatives were only part of a melange of peace probes by scores of would-be mediators from dozens of nations. According to Johnson, the United States was in virtually continuous contact with Hanoi from 1965, either directly or through intermediaries; there was also no shortage of self-appointed mediators who often did more to confuse issues than to clarify them:

> We could never be certain whether we were hearing accurate reports of what Hanoi had said — or what Hanoi wanted us to hear — or whether we were hearing wishful thinking about what Hanoi might be willing to do under various circumstances. . . . I learned that everyone who was engaged in such efforts came to think that his own particular approach was the one that would, or should, succeed.[40]

It is not surprising that Ottawa placed much more emphasis on the Canadian initiatives than they ever received in Washington. According to Cooper:

> Washington's view toward "third government" peace efforts was typically a mix of noblesse oblige, diffidence and scepticism. Although the country involved in this initiative regarded its offer to help as a serious, perhaps

129

politically risky matter, to the Administration in Washington it was just the latest in a long series of unfruitful efforts.[41]

With much less tact, Dean Rusk ridiculed the would-be peacemakers in a talk to educators attending a State Department conference in June 1967. According to the official transcript, the Secretary described the peace probes in this way:

Really, what happens on these matters is basically this: There are an awful lot of candidates for the Nobel Peace Prize running around the world these days (laughter and applause). . . . They don't understand what they hear. And if the ladies will forgive me, they frequently come out of Hanoi or some other contact eight months pregnant (laughter); and then when we check it out with Hanoi, we find there's nothing in it (laughter, applause).[42]

With such attitudes at the highest level in Washington, it is no wonder that the Canadian initiatives were never taken seriously. Martin may have seen himself as a candidate for the Nobel Peace Prize, but this in no way detracts from the importance of the message which Pham Van Dong gave to Ronning. If the Americans had paid attention to Martin and Ronning in 1966, they *might* have had negotiations on the same terms which they were forced to concede two years later, after thousands of more deaths, billions of more dollars, horrendous devastation to both Vietnams and incalculable damage to their own society.

Whether or not Hanoi was serious about negotiations in 1966 and 1967, the Americans scorned the Canadian initiatives in a manner that belied their own peaceful pretensions. When all allowances have been made for bureaucratic confusion in Washington — and for American weariness with the multitude of mediators — there is no way to justify Washington's attempts to sabotage or pervert the Canadian moves through premature publicity and military escalation. All it came to in the end — all the hard work by Pearson, Martin, Seaborn, Ronning and numerous other Canadians — were a few cheap jibes by the ineffable Dean Rusk.

But Ottawa was far from blameless. To the very end Canada continued in its role as an undeclared but effective ally of the United States in Vietnam. Pearson and Martin eventually came to believe that the Americans were using unnecessary force to achieve their aims and that their pursuit of total victory involved the unacceptable risk of a wider war. Privately — and finally to some extent in public — they began to urge a halt to the bombing as a first step in a process which would enable the Americans to cut their losses and withdraw. In later years Martin maintained he would have spoken out against the US war as early as 1964 if he had known then that all his Quiet Diplomacy would never succeed.[43]

But Pearson and Martin only came to differ with the Americans over the *means* that they were using in Vietnam; there was never any serious quarrel over the *ends* of American policy. Ottawa never doubted that the Americans had been right to view the insurgency in the South as a form of Communist aggression which threatened the security of the whole Western alliance. Blinkered by Cold War dogmas and insensitive to Asian political trends, the Canadian government never saw any need to challenge the Americans on their basic perception of the conflict and so became fatally entangled in the American escalation.

After making such a whole-hearted commitment to the American cause, the Canadians were both naïve and misguided to think that they could somehow act as peacemakers. With all the evidence of the Seaborn period, it was naïve to believe that the Americans had any serious interest in negotiations before they had brought the North Vietnamese to

131

their knees. It was certainly misguided to think that Canada had sufficient influence in Washington to reverse the ruthless pressures for continued escalation. When Washington finally agreed to stop the bombing and start negotiations, it was for reasons which Hanoi had always anticipated: an American realisation that the war could never be won at an acceptable price and that it was causing dangerous political and social turmoil within the United States. Until then, all the protestations from such allies as Canada, Britain and France — whether they were made in public or in private — had been dismissed as minor and inconsequential irritants.

As the example of France well indicates, Public Diplomacy by Ottawa might have proved equally futile. If Pearson and Martin had openly declared their opposition to the bombing, it might not have halted a single raid. It certainly would have increased Washington's scepticism of any future Canadian peace initiative. To this extent, the Quiet Diplomats have a case.

Since Quiet Diplomacy and Public Diplomacy were *both* likely to fail, it would have been much better for Ottawa to have made clear — in one or two firm public statements by Pearson and Martin — that enough was enough. By the middle of 1966, Canadians had served for 12 thankless years on the ICC — for much of that time as little more than American surrogates. Canadian peace initiatives had either been scorned by the Americans or else perverted to serve their own military ends, and thousands of Vietnamese had been killed with the help of Canadian products. In the eyes of other nations, Canada was at best an apologist for the Americans, at worst an ally of the United States in a barbarous and senseless war. Above all, Canada's acquiescence in the atrocity of the US bombings made a mockery of Ottawa's claims to play a constructive role in support of peace and as a bridge between the rich and poor nations.

Ottawa's failure to speak out also left Canada vulnerable to further American demands. If the government had withdrawn from the ICC when it became moribund — and revoked its support for the American policies when they became tragically irresponsible — the Americans would had had little inclination to seek Canadian help as they finally began to extricate themselves from the conflict, while doing everything else possible to maintain a repressive puppet regime in Saigon.

Instead, as the Paris negotiations neared agreement on a ceasefire, Washington again turned to Ottawa for assistance. By then there was a new Canadian government, with a very different sort of leader *and* a very different style in diplomacy. Its response to the American approach would be marked by those differences; it would also do little to enhance Canada's dwindling reputation as a responsible and fair-minded nation.

four

Canada . . . has fallen into a more modest role,
and it should reassess its foreign policy
rather than trying to peace-keep everywhere,
which, in a sense, means that we're trying
to determine international situations.

Pierre Elliott Trudeau (1968)

If there was every any truth in the conventional view that Canadian politics are dull — and that Canadian politicians are equally uninspiring — the events of 1968 provided clamorous exceptions. As Canadians still basked in the ersatz glow of Expo 67, they became captivated by a new political leader who embodied their desire for a break with the dreary infighting of the Pearson-Diefenbaker era and whose combination of personal glamour and intellectual incisiveness brought a fresh excitement to the old electoral game. From teenyboppers to university professors, the people were seized by Trudeaumania — while there were always sceptics, the craze was strong enough to give the Liberals what they had never achieved under Lester Pearson: a solid majority in the House of Commons. We can now see Trudeaumania as partly the creation of political reporters and party publicists; we now know that the man himself is much more cautious and conservative than many had once imagined. But in 1968 the sceptics were largely ignored and the political atmosphere was charged with the heady promise of new directions.

There was little talk of Vietnam in the 1968 campaign: as usual neither the politicians nor the electorate showed much concern with foreign policy. At the same time, some of the heat had gone out of the conflict: while there was no let-up to the fighting in the South, the bombing of the North had been severely curtailed and it seemed only a matter of time before the Paris talks evolved into serious negotiations. With these developments the Canadian anti-war movement lost much of its impetus. There was little point in urging Ottawa to criticise an American government that seemed bent on winding up the war (or at least its part in the hostilities), nor were there any apparent opportunities for Canadian mediation. Most Canadians had even forgotten that a handful of their compatriots were still serving fitfully on the ICC. With the war no longer dominating their newspapers and television screens, they could almost ignore Vietnam.

But many of Trudeau's most fervent supporters were academics and other intellectuals who were opposed to the Pearson-Martin tradition of Quiet Diplomacy and who favoured a stronger assertion of Canadian interests. For most of them, Vietnam had been the crucial test: they were still angry and frustrated over Ottawa's acquiescence in the American war. These critics were heartened by Trudeau's campaign promise that there would be a "severe reassessment" of Canadian foreign policies. When the Liberals gained

139

their sweeping victory, it was widely noted that Trudeau was the first modern Canadian Prime Minister whose outlook had not been formed by World War Two and who might be less than totally committed to collective security, the Atlantic Alliance and other basic concepts of Pearsonian diplomacy. It was no secret that "Trudeau and some of his closest and most powerful ministerial associates, such as Jean Marchand, Gerard Pelletier and Donald Macdonald, shared, when they came into office, an evident dissatisfaction and even frustration with the foreign policy of the Pearson government."[1]

Only later did it become apparent that this frustration was more involved with the style than the substance of Canadian diplomacy. Impatient with bureaucratic methods and scornful of traditional diplomatic activities, Trudeau was less concerned with charting bold new directions than with circumventing the prestigious External Affairs Department. With Martin elevated to the Senate, his task was relatively easy. For five years Martin had kept firm control over foreign policy, refusing to make concessions to public opinion (especially over Vietnam) and resisting policy changes or reviews suggested by younger ministers such as Trudeau and even, on occasion, by Pearson himself. His successor, Mitchell Sharp, never established such control. A veteran minister from the Pearson era, Sharp had run for the Liberal leadership, throwing his support to Trudeau at the last moment. But the two men were never especially close. In the realm of diplomacy, Trudeau came increasingly to rely on Ivan Head, an Alberta lawyer and former External Affairs officer who became a key member of the Prime Minister's inner circle. Head undertook a multitude of delicate foreign missions for Trudeau and soon became known — by friends and critics alike — as Canada's answer to Henry Kissinger.

Once in power, Trudeau proved to be less daring in revising the *substance* of Canadian foreign policy than some of his supporters had anticipated. As Bruce Thordarson has pointed out, much of the confusion arose from a misreading of Trudeau's views on nationalism and the nation-state. While these views are complex, they have never encompassed an extreme assertion of Canadian nationalism at the direct expense of good relations with the United States. "In general Mr Trudeau views the United States as Canada's best friend and ally − certainly not as an imperialistic power against whom Canada defend itself."[2] But Trudeau was prepared to take decisions which aroused American opposition or apprehension if they seemed essential to Canadian self-interest − for example, the assertion of sovereignty over Arctic waters, the recognition of China and the reduction of Canadian forces in Europe.

Aside from such specific acts, Trudeau's main contribution to the reassessment of Canadian diplomacy was *Foreign Policy for Canadians:* six slim booklets which were published in 1970 after two years of debate and consultation, inside and outside government, and which bore the unmistakable stamp of the Prime Minister's own priorities. As a firm believer in the Canadian nation-state, Trudeau had never been an advocate of Pearsonian internationalism: his new policy made clear that Canada would become more inward-looking, more concerned with developing national unity and less eager to accept international commitments. The paper took a much more modest view of Canada's world role than Pearson or Martin had ever adopted: specifically it rejected their tendency "to base foreign policy on an assumption that Canada can be cast as the 'helpful fixer' in international affairs." On peacekeeping, the new policy was equally explicit:

> There could be further international demands for Canadian participation in peacekeeping operations − especially in regional conflicts. The Government is determined that this special brand of Canadian expertise will not be dispersed or wasted on ill-conceived operations

141

but employed judiciously where the peacekeeping operation and the Canadian contribution to it seem likely to improve the chances for lasting settlement.[3]

It seemed clear that Trudeau and his advisers regarded Canada's lengthy involvement in Vietnam as one of those "ill-conceived operations" which was not to be repeated. After all the furor of the previous decade, Indochina received less than a page in the Pacific booklet of the foreign policy review. With the Americans and the North Vietnamese making little progress in their Paris talks, the authors took an extremely cautious view of any future role for Canada. In the event of a clear settlement of the conflict, Canada might participate in a supervisory role, "provided that a clear mandate, adequate resources and the full co-operation of the parties could be assured." Even this tentative commitment evoked unease in the authors, since they went on to warn that "it would be unwise for Canada to go any distance in advance toward undertaking a new obligation to supervise a political settlement until it has been fully defined and is judged acceptable and workable."[4]

Sympathetic critics like Thordarson maintain that Trudeau was never concerned to downgrade peacekeeping but only to assert that future ventures had to have a reasonable chance of success in order to avoid the fate of the ICC. "Above all, the Prime Minister wanted Canadians to realise that foreign policy should be based on the quest for specific national goals rather than on a vague desire to achieve prestige and glory."[5]

Others were more sceptical about Ottawa's ability to overcome instinctive habits. Watching events from his embassy in Washington, the veteran Canadian diplomat Marcel Cadieux warned that Canadians might well react to a request for a new peacekeeping role in Indochina like an old race-horse to a track, and be unable to restrain themselves from having another run.[6]

As it turned out, Cadieux was right. But when Canada undertook its new commitment in Vietnam, it *was* for "specific national goals" — at least as Trudeau saw them.

* * * * *

Ottawa protested too much. As a new peace agreement slowly emerged in Paris, Trudeau and Sharp in particular began to sound like skittish schoolgirls who keep proclaiming "No, no, you mustn't!" as they summon up the courage to spread their legs for yet another time. After the event there would be talk of rape — another schoolgirl trait. But Ottawa was resigned to its fate, if not exactly overjoyed about the prospect, and it was even prepared to seek its own perverse pleasure in the act.

For a long time, however, the government gave the impression that it was determined to impose tough conditions before it accepted another peacekeeping mandate. In early 1969, Sharp was already warning that Canada would think twice before joining any new truce commission in Vietnam. In January 1970, the cabinet decided that Canada would only join a new commission if it could play a genuinely useful role:

> It was the view of the Government that Canadian participation should make a real contribution to peace and orderly political and economic development in the area, that no commitment should be of indefinite duration, that the supervisory organization should have adequate resources for its work and immediate access to any part of the territory to be supervised, and that its reports should go to a continuing political authority which would make them public, as might any of the participating supervisory powers.[7]

These conditions reflected Canada's sad and frustrating experience on the ICC. Within External Affairs they were seen as

143

the bare minimum upon which Ottawa had to insist. Significantly, the Department's attitude was shaped by the scores of diplomats who had already served in Indochina and who were virtually unanimous in opposing a new Canadian involvement on almost any terms. Still proud of their performance under impossible conditions and still largely unrepentant of their hard-line views, they were determined that Canada should not suffer further humiliation at the hands of Communists and weak-willed neutralists. In the months ahead they would struggle against any new Canadian commitment; when they lost that battle, they would work just as hard to ensure a speedy Canadian withdrawal from the new commission by demonstrating and proclaiming its blatant weaknesses.

For Ottawa the crunch came in late October 1972. The government had long realised that its experience in Indochina made it a prime candidate for any new truce commission. But the first official notification came on October 25, when Secretary of State William Rogers phoned Sharp to tell him that "Canada's name is in play" in the Paris talks. In a statement later that day, Sharp said that Canada had not yet received a formal invitation, adding: "It is possible that we will be asked to play some part in a peacekeeping role and we have said that we would look sympathetically on it as long as it is not a farce like the ICC."

On the morning of October 26, Rogers summoned Cadieux to inform him that both sides in Paris had agreed on a new international commission comprising Canada, Indonesia, Poland and Hungary. At the same time, other Canadian officials received a very skimpy briefing on the new commission's mandate from William Sullivan, one of Roger's senior deputies. Later that day, Kissinger announced that peace was at hand in Vietnam.

Although the government was hardly taken by surprise, it continued to react cautiously. At a press conference in

144

Toronto — where he was in the last throes of the election campaign — Trudeau said that Canada would join the new commission only if it was sure of playing an effective role. On the same day, External Affairs invited Defence Department officials to form a joint task force to study the question. On the next day, the Defence Department announced it was examining contingency plans for dispatching the Canadian Airborne Regiment to Vietnam in the event of a cease-fire.

At that point it seemed all over bar the shouting. But there were a few nagging problems: peace *wasn't* at hand (Kissinger was soon back negotiating in Paris after a flurry of recriminations between Hanoi and Washington) and Canada had still not announced its formal agreement to participate on the new commission.

It was hardly a time for Ottawa to give serious consideration to a major international commitment. The election of October 30 failed to give a majority to any of the parties; it left Trudeau and his colleagues preoccupied with clinging to power. But the government was neither totally disorganized nor unprepared: aside from the highly sceptical External Affairs officials with their tough position papers on a new peacekeeping role, it also had Ivan Head who could be released from the job of writing Trudeau's campaign speeches and returned to the more congenial task of negotiating with his American *alter ego*, the ubiquitous Henry Kissinger, now jetting back and forth between Washington and Paris. Not for the first time, however, Head and External Affairs failed fully to co-ordinate their efforts — this would prove a further source of confusion in the weeks to follow.

On November 2, Sharp announced that Canada was prepared to make *some* contribution to peacekeeping in Vietnam. For a start it would make available to any commission — and for a limited period — its 19 ICC delegates who remained in Saigon and Hanoi. Any further commitment would

145

depend on the precise terms of the new commission's mandate. But after a mid-November meeting between Sharp and Rogers in New York, a Canadian spokesman said there was still very little hard information about Canada's projected role.

By now even the average newspaper reader could surmise that Canadian was being railroaded into a new commitment without knowing very much about it. With a brave show of determination, Sharp outlined Canada's basic conditions at a November 21 press conference. These closely followed the original cabinet decision of 1970: Canada would insist on freedom of movement to investigate in all parts of South Vietnam as well as an international authority to which the commission could report. Reporting procedures had to be "workable" — in other words there must be no unanimity rule, especially for reports on truce violations. There would have to be a precise time limit on Canadian involvement, so that Ottawa wouldn't be taking on another open-ended commitment. As another result of the ICC experience, Ottawa was also insisting that all four belligerents had to request Canada's participation, so that Ottawa wouldn't seem to be acting solely for the United States.

That sounded strong enough, but it failed to lighten the gloom which had already settled over External Affairs. Even more than the average newspaper reader, the foreign service officers had reason to believe that their government would eventually settle for much less than it was publicly demanding. Months before, some of the Indochina veterans had anticipated that Canada would again be pressured into joining another toothless truce commission. Hoping to forestall any further humiliation, they set to work on a draft protocol for the new supervisory body. This took many long sessions to complete and involved the ICC veterans in the masochistic pleasures of delving into their personal experiences to recall every loophole, dodge and ploy which the Poles and the Vietnamese Communists had ever used against them. In its final form, their 73-clause document set out terms and conditions which were much more detailed and stringent than any that were ever announced by Sharp. If accepted in Paris, it would have resulted in a peacekeeping force with real powers and built-in guarantees against obstruction.

Several weeks before the Americans informed Ottawa that Canada was a prospective member of the new commission, External Affairs sent its draft protocol to Washington on an unofficial basis, along with one diplomat and one military officer to explain its terms. But the Canadians were dismayed when the Americans failed to understand the reasons for many of the carefully worded provisions. It became obvious that the Americans had learned nothing from the ICC experience and were prepared to settle in Paris for another commission with an equally ineffective mandate. It was also evident that Kissinger had imposed such tight security on the negotiations that the Canadians would have little opportunity to make any real contribution to the final protocols: they were shown only a few tentative paragraphs from the various American drafts and they soon realised that even the State Department experts who were preparing these paragraphs had no idea of the broader context.

While this was a disillusioning experience, few of the Canadians had really expected that the Communist side in Paris would approve an effective mandate for a new truce commission — even if the Americans had been prepared to demand one. For most of the Canadians, their draft protocol was designed to give Ottawa an honourable and compelling reason for saying "no" to Washington's inevitable request.

When that request was made — and Trudeau and Sharp indicated that Canada would make a positive contribution to a new truce — the Canadian officials became convinced that Ottawa would never insist on the terms of their draft protocol, or even stick to the more general conditions which had long been the government's public policy. When the draft

147

protocol was officially conveyed to Washington in late November, it already seemed too late in the day for the Canadian terms to receive a sympathetic study, especially since American officials had already revealed their insensitivity to the finer points which the Canadians regarded as crucial. Furthermore, reports from Paris at the time indicated that the Americans were having enough trouble with the North Vietnamese in the resumed negotiations — they were unlikely to add to their problems and jeopardize an overdue agreement by insisting on the tough supervisory powers which the Canadians were suggesting, especially since Hanoi wanted only a token international presence in the South.

It was also evident that Washington was taking Canada's participation for granted and showing little interest in Canadian sensitivities. From the start, American pressure was intense. Washington implored Ottawa not to hesitate, since a peace agreement was imminent: an assurance which soon proved be be false. In mid-November, a State Department spokesman said that Canada, Indonesia, Poland and Hungary had all agreed in principle to join the new commission; External Affairs tartly reminded Washington that Canada had still not made a firm commitment. The Americans then told Ottawa that Indonesia, Poland and Hungary had already agreed to serve and that Canada was the "missing piece in the puzzle" — but when Ottawa checked with the other three capitals it discovered that this was also far from true. In another clumsy deception, the Americans assured the Canadians that they had tried hard to find a substitute member but that Canada was the only other Western or Western-leaning nation acceptable to Hanoi. After repeated prompting from the dubious Canadians, Washington finally admitted that only one other country — Japan — had even been considered. In the face of such heavy-handed treatment, External Affairs officials became convinced that their battle was already lost.

While the diplomats were gloomy and despairing, there was something close to jubilation at the Department of National Defence. Although the generals had no illusions about the difficulties of peacekeeping in Indochina, they were delighted at the chance to give their men some valuable experience in the field. While it wouldn't be war — the government was even insisting that Canadian peacekeepers shouldn't carry any weapons — it would be much more meaningful and serious for the soldiers than drilling and manoeuvring at home. By this time, too, the military had long since overcome its initial resistance to peacekeeping duties, seeing them as a respectable and prestigeous part of its general role. In November, television viewers saw films of 200 Canadian officers receiving their immunization shots. Such an excess of enthusiasm embarrassed the Prime Minister's Office — in a polite but firm phone call, the generals were told to cool it for a while.

If the generals had few doubts about the cabinet's ultimate decision, Sharp was still maintaining on December 3 that the government had yet to make up its mind and that it would not do so until the ceasefire negotiations had been completed and full information was available on the proposed arrangements. By then there were few politicians or officials in Ottawa who took Sharp's pronouncements at their face value. Five days later, Rogers indicated that he considered Canada's conditions to be reasonable, adding: "We can accept most of them." It seemed clear — especially after Rogers' statement — that *all* of Canada's conditions would never be met, but that Ottawa would hardly refuse to join the new commission at the last moment.

The last moment was again postponed when the Paris talks broke down in the middle of the month. This was followed by American bombing of North Vietnam from December 18 to 30. On January 5, the House of Commons gave unanimous approval to a government motion which deplored the bombing, welcomed its halt and requested the United States to refrain from any further attacks.* Although Sharp qualified the criticism by also deploring North Vietnam's intervention in the South, this was the strongest official Canadian condemnation of any American action in Vietnam. It may have helped to ease the consciences of those MPs who had long been restless over Canada's support for American policies, but it came too late in the war to have any practical effect. By then the negotiations had been resumed in Paris and were clearly on their way to a speedy conclusion.

If there was any anger in Washington over the resolution, it must have been mollified by Sharp who chose the same debate to indicate that the government was resigned to serving on the new truce commission, at least for a limited period. Significantly, he back-tracked on one condition which Ottawa had always professed to regard as essential: the establishment of a "continuing political authority" (CPA) which would be responsible for the peace settlement and to which any of the commission members could report. Newspaper stories from Paris had indicated that there would be no such authority, although an international conference would be convened 30 days after a ceasefire. According to Sharp, Canada would now be prepared to consider serving on the commission for a minimum of 60 days, during which time the results of the international conference would be known. If the conference failed to create a CPA, Canada would reserve the right to withdraw at any time.

In a further indication that Canada was watering down its conditions, Sharp raised the possibility that the new commission might be bound by a rule of unanimity, despite

---

* Diefenbaker was not present for the vote. Earlier that day he had questioned the wisdom of criticising "our great neighbour to the South".

Ottawa's strong objections. In that case the government would feel free to make public any or all of the commission's deliberations. In other words, if the Poles and Hungarians tried to hinder investigations or reports of North Vietnamese violations of the new ceasefire, the Canadians would tell the whole world. This was the origin of Ottawa's "open mouth" policy which was later to become so controversial.

By now only a congenital idiot could assume that there was any chance Canada would not join the new commission. But the farce had to be played out: on January 16, Sharp maintained that Ottawa was still waiting to see the terms of reference before announcing its decision. Sharp gave a similar assurance on January 23, but on the same day Washington announced that the Paris Agreement had been concluded. Drafted at a time when Sharp was denying any such Canadian undertaking, the Agreement explicitly named Canada as a member of the International Commission of Control and Supervision.

* * * * *

It was 1954 all over again. Once more, Canada had been named to a truce commission in Indochina before it had given its formal consent and before it knew the terms of its mandate. As yet another indication of Washington's indifference to Canadian sensitivities, Rogers summoned Cadieux — as well as the Indonesian, Polish and Hungarian ambassadors — and gave them copies of the Agreement 15 minutes *after* the State Department had released embargoed copies to reporters, and only 45 minutes before Kissinger read out the whole Agreement at a Paris press conference. In a further humiliation, Canadian officials in Paris had to scurry in search of Nguyen Thi Binh, the Foreign Minister

151

of the Provisional Revolutionary Government*, and sheepishly ask her for a formal invitation to join the ICCS, so that Canada could maintain the illusion that it was the enthusiastic choice of all four belligerents.

As also happened in 1954, Ottawa had to accept a mandate which was weak and imprecise and which seemed certain to result in stalemate and discord. Putting on a brave front in the House of Commons, Sharp said the draft agreement showed that the belligerents had gone some way to meeting Canada's conditions. But he conceded that the lack of a CPA was a weakness and that the inclusion of a unanimity rule was an "invitation to paralysis".

Officials in External Affairs were dismayed by the new protocols; one ICC veteran referred to "loopholes you could drive a truck through". One of the most serious loopholes was the failure to grant the ICCS complete freedom of movement. This had been a major concern of the old ICC hands who had written the Canadian draft protocol, which called for "immediate and unrestricted access to, and movement within, any or all areas related to (the commission's) responsibilities." But the Paris Agreement merely said that the teams should be allowed "such movement for observation as is *reasonably required* for the proper exercise of its functions" (italics added). The Canadian draft specified that commission teams should have the use of "any and all means of transport" as well as such facilities as bridges and roads. But the Paris protocols contained a much vaguer provision that the commission might use "the means of communication and transport necessary to its functions."[8]

---

* The Provisional Revolutionary Government (PRG) was formed in June 1969, combining the Communist-dominated National Liberation Front and the Alliance of National, Democratic and Peace Forces, an anti-Saigon group which had been formed among intellectuals and other city-dwellers in the wake of the 1968 Tet Offensive.

The Canadian draft would have given ICCS members full diplomatic immunity; the Paris Agreement only granted them immunity "while carrying out their task" — an ambiguous qualification which would prove crucial when the PRG detained two Canadian officers in June. The new commission would also have only 290 diplomats, military officers and support staff from each of its four members: a total that was plainly insufficient to exercise effective supervision over South Vietnam's difficult terrain, long borders and coastline.

In another echo of 1954, Sharp told the Commons that "it is no secret that we have serious doubts about what we are being asked to undertake." But the Paris conference — like its predecessor in Geneva — had presented Ottawa with a *fait accompli*. The ceasefire was due to be signed in Paris on January 27; within hours of that ceremony the first Commission members were meant to be arriving in Saigon. If Canada refused to take part until it had fully studied the Agreement, it risked delaying an end to the fighting. So Sharp could only repeat that Canada was accepting a commitment to serve for an initial 60 days, while announcing that an advance group of Canadian truce observers would be ready to leave by the following weekend.

To most Canadians who had followed the intricate twists and turns of Sharp's pronouncements, it appeared that their government had been bluffing all along — insisting on stringent conditions for joining the Commission and then meekly succumbing to pressure from Washington. In External Affairs, many peacekeeping and Indochina experts thought that the government could have avoided being named to the Commission if it had only taken stronger steps during the previous autumn: announcing the full details of Canadian conditions and making clear that these were not negotiable. Instead it seemed that the government had failed to take issue with the Americans when they began to dissemble and prevaricate, convincing Washington that Canada's conditions

153

were not meant to be taken seriously and that Ottawa was bound to fall into line.

But it would be wrong to make out the Americans as the ruthless villians of the piece, while casting the Canadians in the role of well-meaning but weak-willed patsies. In fact, there were *three* main factors at work in the crucial period from October to January: each played its part in the final Canadian decision to accept membership on the ICCS.[9]

One factor was direct pressure from the United States. This pressure was both intense and clumsy; it led many Canadian officials to speak angrily of American duplicity and heavy-handedness. But American pressure was probably the least important element in the situation.

A second factor was *muddle*. There is always a degree of muddle in any complicated diplomatic process — more so than most diplomats and historians care to admit. In this case, muddle was positively rampant. This was partly a result of Trudeau's tendency to take charge of major foreign policy moves, using Ivan Head as his personal representative, consulting with Sharp but often by-passing the External Affairs bureaucracy and ignoring the rest of the cabinet and the Commons. It was also a result of the political turmoil in Ottawa that followed the October 30 election and the fact that Washington had similiar problems of communication *within* the government.

Head and Kissinger preferred to deal directly with each other, usually on the telephone, and often kept both External Affairs and the State Department in ignorance of their conversations. To make matters worse, there was little love lost between the Prime Minister's Office and the Canadian Embassy in Washington. In his previous job as Under-Secretary (the top career post in External), Cadieux had angered Trudeau and his aides by resisting budgetary cuts which the cabinet was imposing on all the ministries. To no avail, Cadieux had argued that this would mean closing overseas missions and releasing many veteran foreign service officers: in the event, the missions were closed, the diplomats were fired and Cadieux was banished to Washington, from where he regarded Head's ventures in diplomacy with a notable lack of enthusiasm.

At the same time, Cadieux and his senior diplomats were dealing with State Department officials who were seldom close enough to Kissinger to speak with real authority about the Paris talks, especially since Kissinger was obsessed with the need for secrecy. To compound the confusion, the government in Ottawa was still preoccupied with its political survival; it was a rare cabinet member who had Vietnam on his list of priorities. Although Head kept Trudeau informed of all his conversations with Kissinger, External Affairs was seldom fully in the picture and the cabinet was given no opportunity for a serious discussion of whether Canada should join the ICCS.

Despite the muddle, there was always more coherence and conscious direction to Ottawa's actions than was apparent at the time — even though the House of Commons and the Canadian public were never told what was really happening. Far from merely responding to events — including American pressure — the government had a definite policy on Vietnam. This policy governed its actions, not only in the months of October through January, but also through the following six months which ended in Canada's withdrawal from the ICCS.

This was the third and most crucial factor. It sprang from Trudeau's hard-headed approach to foreign affairs and his reluctance to accept the sort of international commitments which Pearson and Martin had so frequently and fervently embraced. Although Trudeau was convinced that Canada would have to play *some* role in the supervision of a new ceasefire, he was equally certain that the truce would soon break down and that the Canadians should be pulled out as quickly as possible.

155

In early October, when agreement in Paris seemed imminent, Trudeau and his advisers reluctantly decided that Canada could not afford to reject *totally* the inevitable American request for assistance. This decision was based on a cool assessment of the government's self-interest. A refusal could be politically dangerous, especially during an election campaign. Although many Canadians would oppose a new commitment in Vietnam (the early mail to Trudeau's office was heavily against it), there would be much greater revulsion if the negotiations broke down and Canadian hesitation seemed partly to blame.

Like Pearson and Martin before them, Trudeau and Sharp saw little point in picking a quarrel with the Americans. If Ottawa refused to help police the new truce, it would be telling the world that the settlement had no chance of working. This would enrage President Nixon — who had staked his reputation on achieving "peace with honor" and securing an American withdrawal. It would also make the Administration and key Congressional leaders even more unsympathetic in the tough economic negotiations that lay ahead.

Trudeau and Sharp decided to accept a new Vietnam role for one reason and one reason only: to help the Americans get out. This would be Canada's contribution to an *eventual* peace in Vietnam, but Ottawa would undertake no long-term responsibility for how the Vietnamese arranged their affairs once the Americans had gone. The government remained deeply sceptical of Nixon and Kissinger's rhetoric: it was certain that any agreement reached in Paris would be little more than a façade to cover the American withdrawal and that the Vietnamese belligerents would soon be back at each other's throats, with the further possibility of renewed American bombing. So it seemed imperative that Canadian peacekeepers should no longer be around when the peace began to crumble. Otherwise the Canadians would again appear to be guardians of an unsatisfactory status quo, as well as agents of the United States. In turn this would adversely affect Trudeau's policy of strengthening relations with other nations as counterweights to Canada's heavy dependence on the United States — in particular, the new rapprochement with China might be placed in jeopardy by a semi-permanent Canadian presence in Vietnam.

The government's decision to accept a new, limited commitment in Vietnam was made *before* Washington began to put on the pressure. When it came, this pressure was a response to Trudeau and Sharp's equivocal public statements: to ease the task of their negotiators in Paris, the Americans wanted a clear and definite Canadian undertaking to serve on a new commission.

In fact the Americans were left in no doubt that *some* assistance would be forthcoming. On several occasions in November and December, this assurance was given by Head to Kissinger and by Sharp to Rogers. But the Canadians refused to make any specific commitment; they also rejected an American suggestion that they should send an observer to the final stages of the Paris talks.

Ottawa was determined to avoid any responsibility for an overall political settlement in Vietnam; it was also trying hard to keep some options open. For a long time — at least until late December — Ottawa even hoped that it might honour its commitment to the United States without joining a new truce commission. This was the basis of Sharp's suggestion on November 2 that Canada might make its ICC delegates available for a limited period. This suggestion was developed into a two-point program: (1) Ottawa would refuse to join a new commission on *any* terms; (2) Ottawa would offer to strengthen its ICC delegation — if necessary with a few hundred additional soldiers and diplomats. This beefed-up Canadian contingent would supervise the American withdrawal in the early weeks of the ceasefire. By that time the new commission would be in a position to start its work with

157

another nation (Norway and Austria were considered possibilities) taking the place originally allocated to Canada.

This ingenious strategem came to grief at the last moment when the government's legal advisers warned that it would be technically impossible to implement. Washington and Saigon would also have strongly opposed such a limited Canadian offer since it would have underlined the real purpose of the Paris negotiations — to get the Americans out of Vietnam — and would have made clear that Ottawa regarded the remaining peace provisions as little more than window dressing. But the fact that the government was considering this plan until almost the last minute is a striking indication of Trudeau's determination to avoid a major new commitment in Vietnam.

In turn this explains why Sharp was at such great pains to keep on restating Canadian terms for serving on a new commission when no one in Ottawa had any expectation that these terms would ever be met. When Canada finally accepted membership on the ICCS, it seemed that Sharp had been bluffing all along and that his bluff had been called — crudely and ruthlessly.

Again, however, there was more purpose to Canadian actions than was apparent at the time. If the ICC stratagem had worked, Ottawa could have refused to join the new truce body for reasons that had long been public knowledge. More important — if Canada finally had to serve on the ICCS, it would only stay on the job as long after the American withdrawal as seemed decent and practicable. At that point Canada would find a pretext for its own withdrawal: the conditions which Sharp had enunciated so frequently *before* Canada joined the ICCS would be used to justify its *subsequent* departure. When those conditions were clearly not fulfilled — and then the truce broke down — the Canadians could take their leave in all good conscience, maintaining that they had done their best and that they were free of any blame. At that stage it would be difficult for the Americans or anyone else to accuse Ottawa of acting in haste, or irresponsibly, or without sufficient warning.

It was a devious strategy — one might almost say devilish (one also wonders what Pearson would have thought of it). For its success it would depend on one further ingredient: a large dose of constant publicity for all the failures and stalemates which — Ottawa was quite convinced — would soon engulf the new commission. But this had also been carefully considered in advance. As the 290 Canadians began arriving in Saigon on January 29, Ottawa had already announced that their leader would be Canada's ambassador to Greece: a 53-year-old career diplomat named Michel Gauvin. What Ottawa failed to disclose — although it soon became evident — was that Gauvin had been especially chosen for his abrasive temperament. As an External Affairs colleague was later to remark: "We sent Gauvin because he's such an arrogant bastard." For better or worse, the Poles and the Hungarians were soon to taste that arrogance.

* * * * *

Gauvin had a reputation as a troubleshooter. On a special assignment to the Congo in 1964, he had negotiated the release of Canadian missionaries held captive by rebels. Less than a year later, he was dispatched to the Dominican Republic to arrange the evacuation of Canadians caught in the midst of another uprising. Earlier in his diplomatic career, he had spent six weeks in Hanoi and nearly a year in Saigon on the old ICC. That was in 1955: the year when everything started to turn sour for the Commission and when its Canadian members became implacably hardened against the North Vietnamese. Of all the possible choices to head Canada's delegation to the ICCS, this tough and volatile Québécois was the man most likely to be impatient with delays in the new commission's work and unsympathetic to Communist points of view.

159

When he took up his duties in Saigon, Gauvin had one main instruction: to follow an "open mouth" policy. Regardless of Communist or Vietnamese sensitivities, he was to speak out — loudly and publicly — whenever the ICCS became deadlocked or otherwise frustrated in its work. By sounding off in public, Gauvin would also be hastening the day when Canada could decently abandon its new commitment: this was the real basis of the policy.

In the first days of the Commission's work, the other three members rejected a Canadian proposal that their meetings should be open to reporters. So Gauvin began to cultivate the large foreign press corps in Saigon. At receptions, dinners and frequent interviews, he would soon be regaling the reporters with pungent comments and detailed stories on the turmoil and disputes within the Commission. Since most of the reporters were from the West, and since the Poles and Hungarians were slow to develop their own press relations, nearly all the stories filed from Saigon reflected Canadian views and portrayed Gauvin as a skillful and colourful battler for the truth amid a cabal of wily and deceitful Reds.

Gauvin and his aides also spoke freely to the Americans in Saigon, giving them full reports on Commission meetings with references to Communist "sophistry" and "obstructionism". In turn, the US Embassy passed on these reports to American newsmen, adding to the general impression that the Canadians were the heroes, and the Poles and Hungarians the villains, of the ICCS. Although Ottawa always maintained that the Canadian delegation was impartial and objective, an American correspondent reported that:

> Canadian delegation members . . . apparently are the chief source for much of the information in the (US Embassy) reports. They seem to be playing to a limited extent the same role for the United States that the Poles and Hungarians clearly do for the PRG.[10]

But Gauvin was more than just a good talker. From the start he took virtual charge of the ICCS and forced the pace of its activities. This was partly because of his driving temperament and partly because the Canadians, with their solid expertise in peacekeeping, had an initial edge over the Indonesians, who were newcomers to the field, and the Poles and Hungarians, who were less well organised and who favoured a more cautious and passive role for the ICCS. As chairman of the Commission in February (the post was to rotate on a monthly basis), Gauvin soon had ICCS teams in all seven regional headquarters designated by the Paris Agreement and was pressing the exchange of prisoners which the Agreement said should be completed within the first 60 days. While Canada's political objectives were always highly dubious, there is no doubt that the Canadians were instrumental in giving the Commission an efficient infrastructure.

But trouble was piling up for the ICCS. While the withdrawal of American troops was working smoothly, the truce proclaimed in Paris was proving to be extremely precarious, with fighting continuing throughout the South as both sides sought to consolidate or extend their positions. By mid-February, Gauvin was publicly criticising the Four-Party Joint Military Commission for failing to fulfil its obligation to establish an effective ceasefire as well as demarcation lines between the belligerents. By the end of the month, ICCS groups were only starting to fan out very tentatively from their regional posts to the 14 team sites from which they were meant to observe violations of the truce, including fighting and infiltration. At the same time, Canadian spokesmen in Saigon were telling newsmen that the ICCS had yet to have any serious, substantive discussions and that Gauvin was looking for a chance to "go public" with a minority report that would criticise the Poles and Hungarians for their stalling tactics.

In these unpromising circumstances, Sharp arrived in Paris for the 12-nation conference which opened on February 26 and which was meant to guarantee the January agreement. In line with Ottawa's "open mouth" strategy, Sharp made clear that Canada still wanted a CPA and was not prepared to remain on the ICCS if the Commission was simply to continue sending its reports to the four belligerents. Instead of this closed-circuit approach, Sharp proposed that the ICCS should report to the UN Security Council, or the UN Secretary-General.

Once again Canada's brave words had little impact. According to press reports, Rogers concluded that Sharp was merely bluffing — at any rate, the Americans were reluctant to give him strong support for fear of precipitating an open conflict with Hanoi and the PRG. In the event, the conference merely decreed that any of the four ICCS members could send reports of ceasefire violations to any or all of the four belligerents who, in turn, would be responsible for passing them on to the other governments who had attended the conference, as well as to the UN Secretary-General. The conference itself could only be reconvened by a joint request of the United States and North Vietnam, or at the request of at least six of its 12 members.*

These cumbersome provisions fell far short of a CPA to oversee the truce. With a show of reluctance and disappointment, Sharp initialled the final declaration, stating that "the spirit of the act and the good will reflected in it were deserving of support", but warning that Canada was not accepting any new responsibilities and still reserved the right to withdraw from the ICCS after the first 60 days. Back in Ottawa in early March, he told MPs that Canada's continued participation would depend on two main conditions: there

---

* The United States, North Vietnam, South Vietnam, the PRG, China, the Soviet Union, France, Britain, Canada, Indonesia, Poland and Hungary.

would have to be greater co-operation within the ICCS over undertaking investigations of reported ceasefire violations, as well as greater co-operation from the belligerents in allowing the Commission access to areas where the violations were taking place.

In other words, it was getting to be like the ICC all over again. This time, however, Ottawa was making clear that there were strict limits to Canadian patience. No one would be fooled or impressed by Sharp's call for greater co-operation, since it was already evident that both Saigon and Hanoi would continue to break the ceasefire whenever it suited them. The Canadian government had no illusions that the Paris Agreement could be made to work: it was simply serving notice that it would pull out its peacekeepers as soon as politically possible. The only question was . . . how soon?

* * * * *

By now the first 60 day period was nearly over: in South Vietnam there was little of the "good will" which Sharp had detected in Paris. As the Canadian delegation reported in a cable to Ottawa:

> It is incontestable that the ceasefire has not, as of March 13, been effective throughout Vietnam. Total of six thousand sixty incidents have been reported between January 28 and March 14. While we have had no indication that American forces are involved in the continuing hostilities, it seems clear from the info we have received that the three Vietnamese Parties are still engaged in hostile activities designed to enlarge their areas of control.[11]

Only a handful of these violations had been officially reported to the ICCS: a sign of the contempt in which both

163

Saigon and the PRG held the Commission as well as an indication of their indifference to its investigations.

As the Canadian report also indicated, the Commission had already become virtually deadlocked along predictable Communist and non-Communist lines. The turning point came in early March, after the Americans announced that the North Vietnamese had installed surface-to-air missiles (SAMs) around their air strip at Khe Sanh in northern South Vietnam. If true, this was a clear violation of the Paris Agreement, but the Poles and Hungarians refused Canadian and Indonesian demands for an investigation, maintaining that the American aerial reconnaissance photographs which had allegedly revealed the presence of the SAMs were themselves a violation of the ceasefire and that there were "inadequate grounds" to justify an inquiry — an argument which the Canadian report described as "specious and unconvincing". While the Canadians felt they had been frustrated by the Communists in undertaking previous investigations, this was the first time they had been unable to get agreement within the Commission to take any action whatsoever in response to a ceasefire complaint.

The Khe Sanh dispute was a turning point in more than one sense. For the first time, Gauvin publicly criticised other members of the Commission (without actually naming Poland and Hungary). The incident also exposed a crucial difference between Ottawa and Washington over the Commission's work. After Nixon hinted that he would resume bombing the North if such violations continued, Rogers announced that the missiles had been removed, adding that Canada's strenuous protests were partly responsible.* But Ottawa wanted no such compliments: an External Affairs spokesman tartly replied that the ICCS had played no part in the

---

* A few weeks later, Washington was to claim that the missiles had been reinstalled.

164

removal of the SAMs and that the incident showed the Commission's role had become superfluous. This was the first public sign that Washington was making strong efforts to ensure that Canada remained on the Commission after the initial 60 days, if only to preserve the already tattered illusion that the Paris Agreement still had some chance of working and that Nixon and Kissinger had achieved their much heralded "peace with honor". On March 12, Sharp confirmed that Canada was under "very great pressure" to remain on the ICCS, although he added that the pressure was coming from many other countries as well as the United States.

In response to that pressure — as well as to growing unrest within the House of Commons — Sharp and several MPs visited both Saigon and Hanoi between March 13 and 18 to assess the general situation, the Commission's work and Canada's participation.* From Gauvin and members of his delegation, the visiting Canadians heard the sad story of the frustrations and deadlock on the ICCS; from leaders of both North and South Vietnam, they received formal assurances of support for the ICCS but little indication that either side was interested in the Commission's investigative role.

Back in Canada, Sharp avoided any criticism of Saigon, while attacking Hanoi and its Communist allies on the Commission. He told the House of Commons that information gathered on his trip tended to confirm that thousands of North Vietnamese troops had infiltrated the South since the ceasefire, but that the ICCS had not been permitted to investigate this influx. There had also been thousands of incidents since the Agreement was signed, some involving large-scale operations, but only a few of these had led to

---

* It was meant to be an all-party delegation: although there were Liberal, New Democrat and Social Credit members, the Conservatives declined to send a representative, maintaining that the trip was merely window dressing.

requests for investigations by the ICCS. In a speech in Toronto, Sharp said it was only an "amiable eccentricity" to expect that the Commission would effectively watch over the truce. At the same time, Gauvin was becoming even more open-mouthed in Saigon, accusing the Poles and Hungarians of violating the Paris accords by withdrawing their military observers from Commission team sites at Tri Ton and Ben Cat* and telling an interviewer that the ceasefire was not working.

An innocent observer might have concluded that Ottawa was preparing to announce its withdrawal from the Commission. Instead Sharp told the House of Commons on March 27 that Canada would remain on the ICCS for a second 60-day period — until the end of May. It would then announce its withdrawal — giving a 30-day grace period until the end of June so that a successor could be found — if the present situation continued and if there was no distinct improvement or progress toward a political settlement. "We will not take part in a charade," Sharp warned, "nor will we tacitly condone inaction when we believe action is required." But he added that the situation, although serious, was an enormous improvement over that existing before the ceasefire. The ICCS had justified its existence by providing a framework for the US troop withdrawal and the exchange of American and Vietnamese prisoners-of-war (both of which would be completed by the end of March, although Saigon was later accused of keeping as many as 200,000 political prisoners in brutal and unjustified detention). Sharp also claimed that

* The Poles and Hungarians said they had withdrawn from the two sites, near the Cambodian border, because their safety was in jeopardy. The Canadians charged that the sites had come under sporadic shelling from Communist units because Hanoi was anxious to drive the ICCS teams from the area — so that they could not observe North Vietnamese infiltration — and that Poland and Hungary were aiding this plan. In the following weeks there were similar incidents involving other team sites.

166

Canada's early departure could lead to a resumption of hostilities. He added that similar views had been expressed by both North and South Vietnam, as well as a number of other countries, including the United States, Britain, China and Japan.

This policy statement won support from both the Conservative and Social Credit parties. Without explicitly rejecting the government decision, Doug Rowland, a young New Democrat who had accompanied Sharp to Vietnam and had been visibly depressed by what he had heard, expressed doubts about keeping the option open after a further 90 days. Earlier, Rowland had stated that the prospects for peace were minimal and that there was virtually no chance of the ICCS being able to carry out its stipulated duties. For the moment, however, and barring any catastrophe to members of the Canadian delegation, the minority government could draw a fairly easy breath, knowing that a confused and divided opposition was unlikely to topple the Liberals over their renewed Vietnam commitment.

Once again there had been heavy pressure from Washington — much heavier than Sharp was prepared to admit. Although the Americans had no illusions that the Paris Agreement could be made to work, they were badly troubled by the thought of the domestic and international outcry that would occur if full-scale fighting broke out immediately after the withdrawal of their troops and the return of their pilots from the North. Canada's continued presence on the ICCS might keep the doubters quiet for a while, but a Canadian withdrawal could easily precipitate a new crisis between the belligerents and cause a total collapse of the Paris framework.

There were similar fears in Ottawa, where Trudeau and Sharp were hardly willing to risk the opprobrium that would be lavished upon them — both in the House of Commons and from Washington — if a Canadian withdrawal was immediately followed by a complete breakdown in the truce, leading to

167

charges that Canada had not tried hard enough. The government also realised that in its zeal to avoid a long-term commitment to the ICCS, it had made a tactical mistake in agreeing to serve for only 60 days. This period coincided exactly with the time allotted for the American military withdrawal. If the Canadians pulled out immediately after the last American troops had left the South — and the last US prisoners had been returned from the North — Ottawa could be accused of having joined the ICCS merely to serve the interests of Washington. This *was* the case — given the fact Ottawa had decided that serving the interests of Washington was also the best way of serving its own interests — but in view of the rising tide of nationalist feeling in Canada, the government could not afford to acknowledge the real basis of its policy.

Again there was a strong element of deception in Ottawa's public position. There was never any chance that Canada would pull out after the first 60 days; now it was almost as certain that Canada's withdrawal would be announced by the end of the second two-month period. While Sharp might warn that Canada would not participate in a charade, his earnest words about the need for an effective ICCS were little more than pious hypocrisy. By the end of March, it was quite clear that the Paris accords were foundering and that Hanoi and Saigon were still implacable adversaries. At that point, the last thing that Ottawa wanted was any change for the *better* in the Commission's role, since this would have meant an extended Canadian commitment. Rather, the government was determined that further frustrations and disputes — well publicised and to some extent provoked by Gauvin — would soon provide the excuse for Canada's final and carefully prepared withdrawal from the wreckage that was Vietnam.

* * * * *

168

On April 7, an ICCS helicopter on its way to a team site near the Laotian border was shot down by Communist fire. There were nine men on board and all were killed in the crash: Captain Charles Laviolette of the Canadian Army, one Indonesian and two Hungarian truce observers, two PLA liaison officers, a Filipino flight mechanic and two American pilots working for Air America, a charter company which often undertook clandestine missions for the Central Intelligence Agency and which — somewhat incongruously — was also handling most of the Commission's air transport. There was another UH-1 Huey helicopter on the flight to Lao Bao, a former French customs post on the Laotian border about 20 miles below the demilitarized zone in South Vietnam. The second helicopter was also fired upon and forced down; its crew and passengers escaped serious injury but were detained by a PLA unit.

This was to become the most celebrated and controversial incident during Canada's six months on the ICCS. Before it was finally wrapped up in an untidy and inconclusive report at the end of May, it had widened the ideological split on the Commission and involved Gauvin and the Communists in a welter of insults and vituperation. In retrospect it would seem that some such incident was always inevitable: by early April the ICCS was approaching stalemate with the Poles and the Hungarians increasingly critical of the Canadians and Gauvin more than ready to reply in kind. With the downing of the helicopter, the lid blew off.

Much of the trouble sprang from the fact that Ottawa had its own ideas about the Commission's role: ideas that were shared by none of the other members or any of the three remaining belligerents. For the Canadians were quite alone in wanting to act according to the rule book. In the words of a British observer, they had come to Vietnam

... determined to police the fragile ceasefire on their own terms or not at all. Impeccably dressed in berets, green shorts and knee-length socks, which earned them the nickname "White knees" among the Vietnamese, they looked like a team of international Scoutmasters. And that is rather how they behaved. Sticking strictly to the letter of the Paris ceasefire agreement, they bent over backward trying to be impartial, blowing whistles at anyone who continued fighting. In the context of Vietnam, which has seen a quarter of a century of almost uninterrupted war, it was too much to expect either side to pay any attention to Canada's refereeing.[12]

The Canadian approach always veered between the quixotic and the futile. It was ingenuous of Sharp to tell the House of Commons on May 29 that "what we sought to ensure was that the new international commission would be an impartial, fact-finding body . . . I assure the House that we have no need to listen mutely now or later to any charges that we have acted partially; we can be proud of our objectivity. . . ." It was equally ingenuous for the Canadians to point out that they had blamed the South Vietnamese for ceasefire violations in about 10 of 150 completed investigations and would undoubtedly have blamed them more often, if only the PRG had made more complaints.* It was ingenuous because it overlooked the fact that objectivity was the last thing expected from the Canadians by any of the other parties, especially the Communists.

---

* According to Gauvin, there were relatively few PRG complaints because the Communists lacked sufficient cadres to deploy at all the Commission team sites. Other Canadians speculated that since the Communists were determined to overthrow the Saigon government by force, they had little reason to build up the Commission's supervisory role. But this is only part of the story. Most of the team sites were in areas controlled by Saigon: the PRG charged that when it *did* deploy its cadres, they were often killed by the South Vietnamese, or at least marked for future reprisals, and that the ICCS was powerless to protect them.

To the Poles and the Hungarians, it was stupid and il-logical to talk about objectivity or impartiality. They argued frankly that they were Hanoi's choices for the Commission and that their job was to advocate the cause of the PRG. As the choice of Washington, Canada and Indonesia should be advocates of Saigon. Given this inevitable polarity, they saw little point in investigating violations of the ceasefire: a futile exercise which would only increase tensions on the Commission and in the country. Rather, the Commission members should act as mediators, seeking to restrain the two sides instead of endlessly and tiresomely trying to catch them out in cheating.

But the Canadians had no desire to be mediators or arbitrators. Although they were quite ready to criticise Saigon on occasion, they rejected any larger, more ambitious role which would have enmeshed them indefinitely in the murky issues of Vietnamese history and Vietnamese politics. It was never stated openly — but always quite evident — that by sticking to the rule book and blowing their whistles whenever possible, the Canadians were also driving the Commission into deadlock and hastening their own departure. This, of course, was quite deliberate.

The Indonesians usually sided with the Canadians, but often slowly and reluctantly and with reservations that exasperated Gauvin. It was hard for the Canadians to anticipate Indonesian reactions, partly because Jakarta had sent a divided delegation to Saigon. Many of its military members were veterans of the 1965 counter-coup which had deposed President Sukarno and massacred Communists by the hundreds of thousands; they seemed to embrace their Vietnam assignment as another anti-Red crusade. But some of the Indonesian diplomats were more cautious and flexible; since it appeared likely that Hanoi would end up controlling the South, they were reluctant to be too outspoken against North Vietnamese and PRG violations (although the Canadians would eventually go home, the Indonesians were part of Southeast Asia and had to live with the consequences of the war). The Indonesians were also instinctively inclined to *musjawarah:* an elusive concept which involves a great deal of talk, an avoidance of sharp confrontation and the eventual emergence of a consensus. This approach was probably well suited to the complexities of peacekeeping in Vietnam; it certainly made the Indonesians uneasy allies of the Canadians with their pushy and self-righteous approach.

While the Indonesians urged caution, Gauvin seemed to regard the downing of the ICCS helicopter as a personal affront, as well as a clear example of Communist perfidy. One week later, when the Commission had barely begun its investigation of the incident, Gauvin issued a "considered statement" in which he maintained there was a strong possibility that the helicopter had been shot down by troops "whose presence is not provided for in the Paris Agreement". He added: "We have strong reason to believe that in other parts of South Vietnam, as well as in the area where the helicopter incident took place, non-South Vietnamese troops are infiltrating South Vietnam for the purpose of supporting militarily one of the two parties in South Vietnam."

In other words, Gauvin was not only saying that the helicopter might have been shot down by North Vietnamese troops rather than a PLA unit (which was certainly possible) and that the North Vietnamese were infiltrating South Vietnam to support the PRG (which was true), he was also implying that *none* of the North Vietnamese had any right to be in the South. This was highly contentious. While the Paris Agreement prohibited any infiltration of reinforcements into the South, it did not require Hanoi to withdraw an estimated 145,000 of its troops who were already there. In public statements, Kissinger had made clear that while the United States and South Vietnam did not acknowledge the legality of this North Vietnamese presence, both sides had tacitly accepted the fact when they signed the Agreement. By saying — in effect — that all the North Vietnamese should go home, Gauvin was coming very close to supporting the demands of Saigon, which was trying to set their withdrawal as a precondition for elections and a general political settlement.

This was hardly objectivity or impartiality. Since Gauvin's statement was released to the world press before the ICCS had fully investigated the incident, it struck the Communists as a deliberate attempt to raise a highly sensitive issue in a blatantly partisan manner. To make matters worse, the Canadians in Saigon — and External Affairs officials in Ottawa — were giving currency to American allegations that the wreckage of the helicopter had been moved several miles in order to support Communist claims that it was well off course. Radio Hanoi soon accused Gauvin of making "unscrupulous statements" and a PRG official said he was trying to slander both the PRG and North Vietnam. The Communists also accused the Canadian envoy of shedding "crocodile tears" and of harbouring "ugly intentions", "dark designs" and "Cold War attitudes".

Amid so much acrimony, it was not surprising that the ICCS was unable to reach a unanimous agreement when it wrapped up its investigation on May 24. There was agreement that the two helicopters *were* well off course when they came under fire (the PRG had warned the Commission that it could not guarantee the safety of its helicopters if they strayed outside the stipulated flight corridors). Canada was alone in blaming the PLA "and/or other troops whose presence in the area where the incident took place is well known" for shooting down the first helicopter with a heat-seeking missile. Although generally agreeing with the Canadian conclusions, Indonesia did not echo the implication that North Vietnamese troops may have been responsible. Hungary and Poland refused to concede that there was conclusive proof that the helicopter had been shot down and suggested that it might have crashed for other reasons, with the Hungarians hinting that the US pilots had deliberately flown off course to use the mission as a spy flight for the CIA.

By that time the Commission was locked in another dispute which was to prove equally acrimonious and even more difficult to resolve. On May 16, Canada and Indonesia declared that North Vietnamese troops had infiltrated South Vietnam since the Paris Agreement. Their report was based on the interrogation of four North Vietnamese captured by Saigon. Again seeking the widest publicity for their views, the Canadians called it a "landmark" case, but the Poles and the Hungarians had refused to take part in the investigation. The Commission was soon deadlocked over how it should be handled, with the Canadians threatening to boycott future meetings unless the ICCS considered the report and the Hungarians accusing Gauvin of using "bullying tactics".

The dispute dragged on for six weeks; aside from its major political implications, it involved highly technical debates over the detailed reporting provisions of the Paris protocols. Throughout this period the ICCS continued to function fitfully at a regional level, but there were no plenary sessions of the Commission's central body in Saigon. On June 30 — his last day as chairman under the monthly rotation system — Gauvin finally broke the deadlock with a compromise which allowed the infiltration report to be sent to the belligerents, but without committing the Poles and the Hungarians to endorse its findings. This was Canada's last important move on the Commission. By then its futility was painfully evident and Ottawa had already announced its decision to withdraw.

* * * * *

Throughout April and May there were rumblings and rumours in Ottawa about disagreements within the cabinet over Canada's Vietnam role. Defence Minister James Richard-

174

son was said to oppose a withdrawal from the ICCS, reflecting military views that it was still a useful exercise for the troops. Energy Minister Donald Macdonald and Industry Minister Alastair Gillespie were also reported to oppose any move which might embitter US-Canadian relations at a time when delicate economic negotiations were pending. On a civil service level, there were similar divisions within the interdepartmental task force which had been set up to oversee the Canadian delegation and whose 30 to 40 members often worked late into the night assessing the latest reports of military harassment or Commission disputes. Here, too, the military representatives argued the case for a continued Canadian role, while officials concerned with economic issues cautioned against upsetting the Americans. But most of the task force were the same Indochina veterans who had pleaded against Canada joining the ICCS in the first place and were now just as vehemently advocating a withdrawal; in the cabinet, Sharp argued their case and Trudeau made it clear that a continued Canadian presence was ruled out by his well-publicised aversion to peacekeeping commitments which had no chance of working.

There was another important factor. By mid-May, Washington was taking a surprisingly relaxed view of the growing prospects for a Canadian pull-out. In their contacts with Canadians, US officials were notably failing to make any strong pitch for continued Canadian participation on the ICCS. This apparent complacency was in striking contrast to Washington's original and strenuous efforts to secure Canadian membership on the Commission, as well as its equally strong pressure in February and March, toward the end of the first 60-day period. At that time, Washington was told bluntly that twice was enough and that Canada wouldn't be pressured again in the same way. Although other factors were probably involved (including the near paralysis of official Washington in the wake of the Watergate disclosures), it seemed that the Americans were showing some belated awareness of Canadian sensitivities, especially after the helicopter crash and at a time when other ICCS helicopters and team sites were also coming under Communist fire.

At any rate, Sharp was able to tell the House of Commons on May 29 that the government had taken a "firm and definite" decision to withdraw from Vietnam. He maintained there had been no improvement in the political situation: the belligerents were still denying the Commission free access to all parts of the country and failing to ask it to investigate ceasefire violations. Although Canada favoured impartial reporting, Sharp added, Poland and Hungary were backing the interests of North Vietnam and the PRG. "The Canadian concept of the functioning of the international commission has not been accepted."

Spokesmen for all three opposition parties greeted the announcement with relief: a sign that a decision to renew the ICCS commitment would have been politically perilous as well as unexpected. Yet one part of the decision came as a surprise. At the end of March, Sharp had announced that Canada would stay on the Commission for another 60 days, plus a 30-day grace period. This would have meant a Canadian withdrawal no later than the end of June. But Sharp now said that the withdrawal would take place one month later — on July 31 — at the request of the United States. According to Sharp, Kissinger had asked him in a telephone conversation to delay the pull-out so as not to complicate the talks he would soon be having in Paris with North Vietnamese negotiator Le Duc Tho — talks that were aimed at saving the fragile ceasefire.

Kissinger had something to offer in return, although Sharp failed to make this public. The Americans had promised that they would never criticise the Canadian move, or indulge in any recriminations, provided that Ottawa agreed to the extra month. Washington lived up to its part of the

176

bargain. At a White House briefing, Kissinger told reporters that although it regretted the Canadian decision, the US understood it. This mild reaction helped to mitigate the fact that Kissinger disclosed the Canadian withdrawal almost one hour *before* Sharp announced it to the House of Commons.

It was another breach of diplomatic etiquette; to the long-suffering officials in External Affairs, it was also the sort of heavy-handed treatment they had come to expect from the Americans. By this time the officials were almost paranoid in their suspicion of Washington. Even after Kissinger's statement, some were convinced that the Americans would make only cursory efforts to find a replacement for Canada and would then come back to Ottawa at the last moment, stating that no other nation was acceptable to Hanoi and that Canada would have to reverse its decision. This fear proved unfounded (Iran eventually agreed to take Canada's place), but it was an apt indication of how the ICCS experience had embittered relations between many US and Canadian officials.

There was one final humiliation for Canada — this time at Communist hands — before it finally withdrew from Vietnam. On June 28, two Canadian Army captains were taken prisoner by a PLA unit in a rubber plantation east of Saigon. It took 11 days before the PRG admitted that it was holding the men and another six days to get them safely back to Saigon amid a spate of angry recriminations. The Canadians had left their team site in Xuan Loc on a show-the-flag trip into PRG territory: although it was not an official mission, the Canadian delegation maintained that truce observers were always on duty and should have diplomatic immunity at all times. The PRG retorted that the Canadians had entered their territory unofficially and illegally, implied that they might have been American spies and maintained that their release had been delayed by South Vietnamese military activity in the area. In turn the Canadian delegation rejected suggestions that the two captains were engaged in improper activities and complained that they had been deprived of their uniforms, subjected to physical violence and political propaganda and taken on forced marches through the jungle while bound by the hands and neck. In a final blast at his Communist adversaries, Gauvin told a press conference that the treatment of the two Canadians was the work of "primitives", adding: "It is only in uncivilised countries that such a thing can happen."

A few minutes later, Gauvin tried to correct his blunder, stating: "When I said this was an uncivilised act, I did not mean that this was an uncivilised country." But the damage had been done. Even allowing for the extreme provocation, Gauvin's statements were unfortunately racist. They came on the day — July 19 — when Gauvin left Saigon for Canada after nearly six months of hard work which had driven him to the point of exhaustion. Strongly emotional and frequently intemperate in his speech, he would have been the worst possible choice for the job — if Ottawa had really intended to play an "objective" and "impartial" role on the Commission. But he was an ideal choice for the "open mouth" tactics that were the basis of Ottawa's undeclared but actual policy of exposing and aggravating the shortcomings of the ICCS so that Canada could be freed of its commitment as soon after the American withdrawal as seemed politically possible. By the time the Canadian troops left Saigon on July 31 — immaculate as always in their dark green shorts and light green shirts — they had established a new reputation for Canadian peacekeepers. This was considerably different from the reputation of quiet efficiency and impartial common sense which previous Canadian contingents had established in Cyprus, the Middle East, the Congo and Kashmir. While efficiency and expertise were still part of the package, notice had been served that Canadian peacekeepers could also be officious and outspoken, as well as short-tempered and self-righteous.

* * * * *

It remained to be seen whether other nations would find
much future use for scoutmasters who were quick to blow
their whistles in delicate situations where patient and painstaking mediation might better serve the cause of peace. It
would also take some time to establish whether Canada — by
sticking rigidly to the rule book in Vietnam — had helped or
hindered the development of peacekeeping as a difficult but
essential diplomatic art. While it could be argued that Ottawa
had made a good case for endowing future peace commissions with mandates that were both precise and powerful, it
was also true that in an imperfect world, where even the
smallest nation stubbornly clings to its sovereign rights, successful peacekeeping still depends more on political sensitivity than cast-iron regulations.

But Canada's role on the ICCS had little to do with
peacekeeping or truce supervision, despite all the anguished
statements by Sharp, Gauvin and other Canadian spokesmen.
Ottawa joined the Commission for its own political reasons:
to help the Americans withdraw their troops, secure the release of their prisoners and cover their Vietnam defeat with
the tattered façade of "peace with honour". The main impulse was always to strengthen Canadian-American relations,
to win a few points for good behaviour.

Yet Canadian participation on the ICCS was never essential to the signing of the Paris accords or to the American
withdrawal from Vietnam. Henry Kissinger is a wily man, and
Washington has many other allies and vassals at its disposal.
Despite the tortuous and prolonged nature of the negotiations, both sides actively wanted the Agreement and the
withdrawal; some other nation could have been found to play
out the charade. If it had been announced early enough and
firmly enough, a Canadian refusal to serve on the ICCS under
any conditions would not have disrupted the Paris negotiations.

179

Indeed, Ottawa likely had an inflated view of its own importance to the settlement. Despite Trudeau's aversion to imprecise international commitments, despite the strong scepticism within External Affairs, there was probably an instinctive feeling in Ottawa that no other nation could match Canada's peacekeeping expertise and that any new truce operation would be unthinkable without Canadian participation. (This certainly seemed to be the case — months after the ICCS fiasco — when Canada appeared desperately to be seeking a berth on the new Middle East peacekeeping force, despite Moscow's opposition and no matter how ignominious the tasks that were eventually assigned to the Canadian contingent.) Old habits die hard — as Cadieux had warned — and pride is the only begetter of many diplomatic disasters.

Yet pride, dignity and self-interest would have been better served if Ottawa had refused to undertake a new role in Vietnam. Although a refusal would certainly have aroused some anger in Washington, it would have saved Canada from the humiliation that was its constant lot after October 1972, and from appearing — yet again — as an American accomplice, no matter how strenuously Ottawa might claim to be impartial.

That was the first mistake. The second was the "open mouth" policy which Ottawa pursued with such a dreary excess of self-righteousness. With their zealous tactics, the Canadians served mainly to exacerbate differences within the Commission and between the warring parties. By seeking to expose and publicise military violations of the ceasefire, they made it easier for Saigon to violate the non-military provisions of the Paris Agreement in which the Thieu government promised vague but positive political concessions which were meant to lead to elections and a new government in which the PRG would be able to participate. In this crucial aspect, the Canadians were decidedly partial in Saigon's favour.

Once committed to a role on the ICCS, Canada would have been more responsible to put away its whistles and its rule book and to work wherever possible for reconciliation and moderation. This would have meant strenuous Canadian efforts to secure the release of tens of thousands of Saigon's political prisoners — many of them leading non-Communists — who remained in brutal captivity in violation of the Paris Agreement. It would also have meant Canadian attempts to prevent Saigon from stalling on the question of free and democratic elections which were also provided for in the Agreement and also made a partial responsibility of the ICCS. By refusing to accept such a larger, political role, Canada was again serving the interests of Saigon and Washington and demolishing its claim to be objective and impartial. With its narrow, legalistic approach, Ottawa decreased the chances for a peaceful solution in the South, and made more likely an eventual resumption of full-scale hostilities. By withdrawing when it did — after acting as it had — Canada was behaving contrary to the interests of the South Vietnamese themselves. It was a sad outcome to nearly two decades in which Ottawa had expressed a constant wish to help the people it was now abandoning.

In the Trudeau era, such humane considerations played little part in the formulation of foreign policy (remember "Where's Biafra?"). Realism was the order of the day. Woolly, Pearsonian concepts of international responsibilities were rigourously shunned. Ottawa went back into Vietnam to help its American friends get off the hook of their obscene involvement. Once the job was done, the Canadians packed their bags and went home again, regardless of the mess they left behind them. It was very neat and very clever. Trudeau and his advisers could even argue that their actions had been highly responsible, since Canada had provided valuable assistance to its most important ally and had helped to arrange the *first* step to eventual peace in Vietnam, although this overlooks the fact that Canadian actions helped to fortify Saigon's repressive power and decrease the chances for political reconciliation.

Critics of Canada's Vietnam policy must beware of trying to have it both ways. In the Pearson-Martin era, Ottawa supported American aims at a time when Washington was constantly expanding the war. Under Trudeau and Sharp, Canada helped the Americans to mask their defeat and withdraw. It is true that this withdrawal had been needlessly delayed — and thousands of more lives had been needlessly lost — through Nixon and Kissinger's determination to leave the Saigon government in a position to struggle on for another year or so. It is also true that the withdrawal was never complete, since Washington continued to prop up the Thieu regime with economic and military assistance, while maintaining strong forces in Thailand as a deterrent to any major Communist military campaign. But it would be inconsistent and illogical to condemn Ottawa for always supporting American policies without making any distinction between Johnson's pursuit of military victory and Nixon's grudging policy of limited disengagement.

While these arguments have some strength, it seems likely that Ottawa's ICCS venture will never rank among the most successful and far-sighted undertakings of Canadian diplomacy. There was too much hypocrisy, too many public protestations of our good intentions, too much striking of holier-than-thou attitudes, too much manipulation of public opinion and the press, too much partiality, too little concern for the Vietnamese themselves — above all, there was too much cynicism. Of all the possible options, Canada chose the worst: accepting a role and then abandoning it as soon as possible, regardless of the consequences and leaving a legacy of bitterness and recrimination.

five

Canada is such a close neighbour that we
always have plenty of problems there.
They are kind of like problems
in the hometown.

Lyndon Baines Johnson

Beneath the skin of every Canadian there
lurks a missionary.

John W. Holmes

At every stage of its involvement in Vietnam, Canada gave active support to the United States and its policies. In the last years of the Pearson government, both Pearson and Martin expressed mild concern about the bombing of the North and launched their own independent peace initiatives despite American reservations. Under Trudeau, Ottawa withdrew from the ICCS somewhat sooner than Washington would have wished. But these differences were minor and inconsequential: for nearly two decades, Canada promoted American interests on successive truce commissions, gave public endorsement to American war aims, provided the Americans with political and military intelligence, became diplomatically entangled in the Americans' escalation policies and fed millions of dollars worth of military hardware into the American war machine. Although Canadian leaders sometimes expressed *private* opposition to specific American actions, their efforts to diminish the warfare or hasten negotiations were a total failure.

It should be stressed that Canadian support was given willingly and often voluntarily. Canada was never a mere victim of intense American pressure, forced into becoming a reluctant ally in Vietnam in order to avert explicit or apprehended threats of American economic retaliation. At most, pressure from Washington was a secondary factor: when the Americans leaned on us, they found that we were already nearly supine.

If Ottawa was such a willing accomplice, it was partly because successive Canadian governments — starting with Mackenzie King's — had so thoroughly entwined Canadian economic, military and diplomatic interests with those of Washington that Ottawa had virtually lost the habit — if not the possibility — of independent action. It was also because Pearson, Martin and other Canadian officials of their generation had an outlook that was based upon their experience of the League of Nations, appeasement, World War Two and its immediate aftermath. Strongly committed to the Atlantic Alliance and collective security, they reacted in terms of European history, with too little understanding of Asian nationalism and Communist polarities and too much readiness to accept the domino theory and other phobias of the Acheson-Dulles tradition of militant anti-Communism. Such attitudes may have been unavoidable in 1954, in the wake of the Korean War, the Berlin blockade and other Cold War shocks. But they were inexcusable by the mid-1960s, when Canadians had been involved in Indochina for a decade but were still repeating the same old slogans, arguing the case of Ngo Dinh Diem or his tawdry successors and failing to perceive that the Americans were merely repeating the disastrous mistakes of the French.

Even when they began to doubt American methods — if not American aims — Pearson and Martin were incurably wedded to the doctrine of Quiet Diplomacy and to Pearson's belief that Canadian-US differences should be played down, and Canadian policies even modified on occasion, because of the effect that open disputes might have on the many problems between the two nations. There was little change from 1951, when Pearson had written privately that "These problems, some of them difficult enough to solve, and which are far more important to us, naturally, than they are to the Americans, make it all the more important that the general atmosphere and general relationship between the two coun-

186

tries should be good."[1] Although the Americans might never be so crude as to offer economic concessions — such as an auto pact — in return for Canadian support in other parts of the world, there was always a feeling in Ottawa that if Canada was difficult over problems which affected vital American interests, Washington would be much less sympathetic when crucial Canadian interests were at stake.

There was also a naïve belief that Quiet Diplomacy could work over Vietnam and that polite but sustained pressure could somehow sway an angry and determined Lyndon Johnson, as well as the powerful phalanxes of Pentagon generals and zealous White House and State Department hawks. It is not even necessary to have the frightening evidence of the Pentagon Papers to know that this expectation was always hopelessly ingenuous: Johnson's humiliating treatment of Pearson at Camp David or the contemptuous mendacity of William Bundy should have been sufficient to convince the Canadians that their efforts to foster negotiations or to restrain the American war machine were certain to fail.

Although Trudeau and his advisers had less faith in the efficacy of Helpful Fixing, and a much more cautious view of international commitments, they also sought the path of least resistance over Vietnam. Their decision to join a new peacekeeping commission was motivated by their desire to avoid a harsh confrontation with Washington and to prove that Ottawa was still a loyal ally. At best, it can be said that the decision was marginally helpful in securing an American withdrawal from Vietnam. At worst, it is arguable that Canada's performance — much more partisan than mediatory — made the chances for a peaceful settlement even more remote and did little to enhance Canada's dwindling reputation as an independent and fair-minded nation. At any rate, Canada's actions on the ICCS were

187

consistent with its long-standing support for American aims, even if these aims had been altered. To the very end, Ottawa was a most willing collaborator.

* * * * *

It is bad enough that Canada's experience in Vietnam was largely a disaster; it would be much worse if Canadians learned nothing from two decades of frustrated peacekeeping, misguided diplomacy and uneasy complicity in an especially nasty and unnecessary war. For a start, our Vietnam experience shows that the Americans have little interest in our earnest expressions of private dissent and scant patience with our polite attempts to sway them from the path of their latest folly. There can be no going back to the atmosphere of the 1940s and 1950s which were the heyday of Quiet Diplomacy between Ottawa and Washington. Now, according to James Eayrs, "the great beast of state has too thick a hide, too many preoccupations of its own, to prick up its ears whenever a Canadian minister sidles into one of the antechambers of power and there, quietly, courteously, diffidently, decorously, recites from his confidential brief his confidential case."[2] Much more relevant for the 1970s is the image of an outraged Lyndon Johnson shaking his fist in the face of an abashed Lester Pearson — while the players have been changed, the game is still a lot too rough for the smooth diplomacy in which Canadian officials have long excelled.

Advocates of Quiet Diplomacy maintain that Pearson's chilling reception at Camp David after his Temple speech helps to make their case. By speaking out in public — however mildly — Pearson not only failed to sway the Americans but also undermined his own position with the President. But it is wrong to conclude that Pearson's reception indicates what *always* happens to Canadian leaders when they so far forget themselves as to speak their minds in public. As James

188

Eayrs has argued, what really upset Johnson was that Pearson acted not so much out of turn as out of character, since he had a reputation for always speaking smoothly. "To act the part of the quiet Canadian, you've got to keep quiet all the time. But if you keep quiet all the time, you won't be heard, and your case will go by default."[3]

It would be unrealistic to dismiss Quiet Diplomacy as a complete failure, while advocating a policy of raucous dissent from every aspect of American policy which offends our sensibilities. This would not only pander to that unfortunate Canadian tendency to preach which overwhelms us on occasion, it would also be highly ineffective. As John Holmes has pointed out, critics of Quiet Diplomacy spoil their case by treating it as a form of immoral behaviour. "Diplomacy is by nature quiet and cannot very well be anything else. Canada would find itself impotent if it insisted on conducting all its diplomacy in the open, when no other country would think of doing so — or of even talking to people who could not keep a confidence."[4]

This is certainly true of Canadian-US relations. Most of the diplomacy between the two countries is over bread-and-butter issues. These issues are so numerous and complex that painstaking negotiations and representations are generally more productive than angry public disputes; a sympathetic State Department is often Ottawa's best advocate in the tangle of government departments and Congressional committees. Even on such economic issues, however, it can pay to go public — if the stakes are high enough. As David Baldwin has argued: "Given that the American public is relatively apathetic toward Canadian affairs and given that the Canadian public is relatively sensitive to relations with the United States, one suspects that on many issues Ottawa could strengthen its bargaining position vis-à-vis Washington by publicity."[5] In other words, a squeaky wheel often gets the grease and nice guys do finish last.

Much of the chummy, cocktail party camaraderie has already vanished from dealings between Canadian officials and their American counterparts. According to two Washington-based scholars: "Current relations between the two countries are marked . . . by greater formality, or even rigidity, on both sides, and a tendency for decisions to be taken at a higher level. With many sets of tough negotiations going on at the same time, the possibilities of open confrontation are increased."[6] The turning point was probably the autumn of 1971 when President Nixon and his Secretary of the Treasury, John Connally, imposed their drastic import surcharge and served notice that Canada would no longer receive special treatment but was being ranked with Japan, Western Europe and other difficult trading partners. In the months and years ahead, it seems likely that Canadian-US relations will be dominated by similar economic issues of major importance to both sides — including the distribution of energy and resources, the extent and nature of American investment in Canada and the limits of Canadian jurisdiction over its continental shelf. It would be unrealistic to expect that these issues will always be resolved through quiet and equitable negotiations. Faced with the overwhelming might of the Administration, Ottawa will almost certainly be compelled to seek Canadian public support for its negotiating stance.

Nor is it likely that Washington will prove more sympathetic over such crucial issues if Ottawa is giving general approval to US diplomatic and military activities in other parts of the world. Canada's long support for the United States in Vietnam failed to win us special exemptions from the Nixon-Connally crackdown of 1971: a clear sign that Washington is a much harsher and more ungrateful place than the scoutmasters in Ottawa have led us to believe.

If Quiet Diplomacy is decreasingly effective, too much of it is also a bad prescription for the general health of Canadian foreign policy. With the help of the Official Secrets Act, it can be used to muzzle the sort of informed criticism that newspapers, opposition MPs, academics and other concerned private individuals might otherwise direct at the mandarins in the Lester B. Pearson Memorial Building. This, of course, is one of its prime attractions in the eyes of foreign ministers and diplomats who have an instinctive feeling that such critics, springing from the ranks of the Great Unwashed, are too clamourous and too ignorant ever to appreciate the subtle demands of their arcane discipline. But secrecy is often used to shroud incompetence and folly. Even worse, the mystique of Quiet Diplomacy is employed by governments to evade their responsibility to take independent actions or to mask their complicity in policies which arouse wide public disapproval.

In the case of Vietnam, Pearson and Martin were always able to plead that too much debate of the issues, or any public criticism of US policies, would only serve to undermine the strenuous efforts which Canada was making behind the scenes to promote negotiations. But we can now see that these efforts were always doomed to failure and that their futility must have been apparent to Ottawa at least as early as the Ronning missions, and probably in the Seaborn period. Rather than acknowledge that the Americans were totally unreceptive to our initiatives — and were even using them to justify further escalation of the conflict — Pearson and Martin found it more convenient to maintain the pretense that they were actively and productively engaged in private diplomacy, so they could avoid the hard alternative of a public dissent from the American war policies.

Occasional dissent has always been a necessary tonic to the Canadian body politic, feeding our sense of national unity and reminding both ourselves and the Americans that we are different peoples, with different historical and ideological traditions, and that we often look with horror at some of the more grandiose and imperialistic aspects of American foreign policy. Again, this is not to advocate strident, self-righteous diplomacy over every American action which annoys Canadians. As John Holmes has warned: "The danger of the new impatience in the country is that Canadians will lose their sense of proportion and the good reputation they have acquired. Whether they like it or not, they are a middle-sized power and cannot get their way by throwing their weight around like a great power or having tantrums acceptable only from an outraged small power."[7]

But there are times — Vietnam was one of them — when Quiet Diplomacy and Helpful Fixing serve only to mask the fact that a *Canadian* policy has long gone bankrupt. The policy should have been scrapped — and could have been scrapped — long before Canada became fatally entangled in the American war. Instead, the illusion of an active and secret diplomacy was employed to hide the nature and extent of our complicity.

* * * * *

Above all, our Vietnam travails should lead us to question some of those basic myths which still make it difficult for us to judge our true place in the world. For too long we have pretended that we could be all things to all men: loyal allies of the United States, good friends to our ancestral nations in Europe, helpful and generous patrons to the poor peoples of the developing world and a force for sanity and common sense in both the Commonwealth and the United Nations. For too long we have aspired to be universally *liked* and too slow to recognise that nearly 30 years of active postwar diplomacy have left a lot of people holding grudges against us. To them, our Helpful Fixing has often seemed more concerned with means rather than ends, as though the process itself was all-important, rather than the consequences, and as though Canada's main interest was to bolster its own self-righteous image.

192

It is strange that this should still happen in the Trudeau era, under a Prime Minister who long advocated more realism and less rhetoric in the conduct of foreign policy. But it takes time to change psychological patterns which have been established over decades and which have their roots in the earliest colonial period. Our outbursts of sanctimonious diplomacy are probably linked in the national psyche to our normal diffidence as a people — providing a release for repressed emotions as well as an antidote to our feelings of inferiority and insignificance, especially in comparison to our more successful and assertive American cousins. Poor relations often seek consolation in the dubious assertion that, of all the family, they have the purest souls and noblest natures.

But we must not expect the *real* poor among the world community to accept without demur our frequent assertions that we are objective and impartial, as well as reasonable and altruistic. From such vantage points as Peking and New Delhi, Lusaka and Santiago, it looks all too often as though Canada is committed by geographic necessity and economic self-interest to be a loyal partner to the United States in all of its imperial endeavours. Advocates of Quiet Diplomacy have long argued that our influence in such far-off capitals depends on the fact that we *do* have good and intimate relations with Washington, and therefore a special ability to influence American policies in the direction of sanity and moderation. But our Vietnam record has exploded this pretension: on any issue which the United States regards as vital to its own interests, Canada has scarcely more clout than Luxembourg or Afghanistan.

It is hard for Canadians to accept this lack of influence and this suspicion of our motives: surely *everyone* must recognise that we are acting for the best. The scoutmaster syndrome or Mountie mentality dies hard. With our white knees and our pure hearts it is difficult for us to realise that other nations might occasionally regard our actions and our motives with mistrust, and that our penchant for proclaiming the undoubted virtue of our viewpoint sometimes fails to endear us to those whose self-interest inclines them in other directions. Our holier-than-thou posture on the ICCS is only a recent example of this tendency to preachify — as well as an indication that we are in danger of becoming the world's most crashing bores.

It might be different if we practised what we preached. With its record in Vietnam, however, Canada is in no position to lecture other nations about their proper course of behaviour, let alone to proclaim its impartiality and objectivity. Because of its involvement in Indochina from 1954 and because of its public support for Washington's policies, Canada must share some of the blame for the dreadful carnage which the Americans lavished not only on Vietnam, but also on Laos and Cambodia.

Canada was always more *involved* in the American war than our leaders cared to admit. This lack of candor made it possible for Ottawa to persist in its bankrupt policy long past the point where realism and self-interest (not to mention self-respect) should have decreed a change of direction. In turn, this unchecked Canadian complicity made it almost inevitable that Ottawa would endorse a new and misguided commitment to the Americans over the ICCS.

In the future, Canadians would be wise to be wary whenever their government fails to stand up and be counted on a major international issue, pleading that this would compromise its secret initiatives. All too often — as Vietnam has shown — secrecy involves a sell-out.

194

CHAPTER NOTES

INTRODUCTION

1. Hugh MacLennan, "Scotland's Fate Canada's Lesson", *Maclean's*, October, 1973.
2. Robert Fulford, "The Oil Issue and the National Spirit", *Saturday Night*, January, 1974.

ONE

1. Paul Bridle, *Canada and the International Control Commissions in Indochina, 1954-1972* (Toronto: Canadian Institute of International Affairs, 1973), p.10.
2. Lester B. Pearson, *Mike: The Memoirs of the Rt. Hon. Lester B. Pearson* Volume One: 1897-1948. (Toronto: University of Toronto Press, 1972), pp.92, 101.
3. Lester B. Pearson, *Mike: The Memoirs of the Rt. Hon. Lester B. Pearson* Volume Two: 1948-1957. ed. John A. Munro and Alex. I. Inglis (Toronto: University of Toronto Press, 1973), p.170.
4. The Senator Gravel Edition, *The Pentagon Papers* (Boston: Beacon Press, 1971), Volume One, p.567. (hereafter "Gravel").
5. John Holmes, "Canada and the Vietnam War", in *War and Society in North America*, ed. J. L. Granatstein and R. D. Cuff (Toronto: Thomas Nelson and Sons, 1971), p.190. See also Donald C. Masters, *Canada in World Affairs: 1953 to 1955* (Toronto: Oxford University Press, 1965), pp.84-85.
6. *The New York Times* edition of *The Pentagon Papers*, written by Neil Sheehan, Hederick Smith, E. W. Kenworthy and Fox Butterfield (New York: Bantam Books, 1971), p.4. (hereafter "NYT"). See also Frances Fitz-Gerald, *Fire in the Lake* (Boston: Atlantic Monthly Press, 1972), p.76.

7. I. F. Stone, "A Reply to the White Paper", in *The Vietnam Reader*, ed. Marcus G. Raskin and Bernard B. Fall (New York: Vintage Books, 1965), pp.161-162. For a contrary view by a Canadian diplomat who served on the ICC, see William E. Bauer, "The Conflict in the Far East", in *The Communist States and the West*, ed. Adam Bronke and Philip E. Uren (New York: Frederick A. Praeger, 1967), pp.158-163.

8. FitzGerald, pp.147-148. See also Jean Lacouture, *Vietnam: Between Two Truces* (New York: Random House, 1966), p.54.

9. Bridle, p.26.

10. *The Globe and Mail*, Toronto: Nov.4, 1965; Feb.19, 1966.

11. *The Globe and Mail:* Nov.20, 1969.

12. *The Globe and Mail:* Jan.29, 1973.

13. Bridle, p.25.

14. FitzGerald, p.260.

15. NYT, p.242.

16. Bridle, p.26.

17. Peter C. Newman, *Renegade in Power: The Diefenbaker Years* (Toronto: McClelland and Stewart, 1963), p.249.

18. NYT, p.234.

19. NYT, p.307.

20. Holmes, p.186.

21. Lacouture, pp.67-68.

22. Department of External Affairs, *Statements and Speeches:* 64/13, 65/4, 65/8, 65/9, 65/16, 66/1.

23. Martin to author.

24. Charles Ritchie, "The Day LBJ Confronted LBP", *Maclean's*, January, 1974.

25. Dale C. Thomson and Roger F. Swanson, *Canadian Foreign Policy: Options and Perspectives* (Toronto: McGraw-Hill Ryerson, 1971), p.130.

26. Martin to author.

TWO

1. *The Pentagon Papers* (Diplomatic Section), Rusk to Lodge, May 1, 1964. (hereafter "Diplomatic Papers"). *Note:* The so-called Diplomatic Section of the *Pentagon Papers* describes moves by Canada and other third parties to bring about a negotiated settlement in Vietnam. At the request of the US government, a US federal court issued an injunction against their publication. A detailed account of the two Canadian chapters was carried in *The Globe and Mail*, July 6, 7, 9 and 10, 1973. Texts relating to the Seaborn missions were published in *The Canadian Forum*, Sept.,1973. The whole section is available for inspection in the Federal district court house in Los Angeles.
2. NYT, p.238. See also Chester L. Cooper, *The Lost Crusade: America in Vietnam* (New York: Dodd, Mead & Company, 1970), p.238.
3. NYT, pp.242-250.
4. Diplomatic Papers: Lodge to Johnson, May 15, 1964.
5. Diplomatic Papers: Ball to Lodge, May 30, 1964.
6. External Affairs officials and G. A. H. Pearson to author.
7. *Toronto Star*: July 6, 7, 9, 1973.
8. NYT, pp.251 and 261.
9. McGeorge Bundy to author.
10. William Bundy to author.
11. Martin to author.
12. Diplomatic Papers: Bundy to Lodge, May 22, 1964; Lodge to Rusk, May 25, 1964.
13. Gravel, Vol. Three, pp.593, 628.
14. Diplomatic Papers: State Department memo, June 1, 1964.
15. Diplomatic Papers: Rusk to Lodge, May 1, 1964.
16. Diplomatic Papers: State Department to US Embassy, Saigon, Dec.3, 1964.
17. Diplomatic Papers: State Department memo, June 1, 1964.

18. Cooper, p.326.
19. Diplomatic Papers: State Department to US Embassy, Saigon, July 11, 1964.
20. Lyndon Baines Johnson, *The Vantage Point: Perspectives of the Presidency, 1963-1969* (New York: Popular Library, 1971), p.67.
21. NYT, p.258.
22. This account of the Tonkin Gulf incident is largely based on Cooper, pp.238-244, and NYT, pp.258-270. See also David Halberstam, *The Best and the Brightest* (Greenwich: Fawcett Publications, 1973), pp.499-503.
23. Gravel, Vol. Three, pp.521-522.
24. Diplomatic Papers: State Department memo, Aug.17, 1964.
25. Diplomatic Papers: State Department memo, Aug.19 1964.
26. Johnson, pp.67-68.
27. Diplomatic Papers: Harriman to US Embassy, Saigon, Dec.3, 1964.
28. Gravel, Vol. Three, p.628.
29. Diplomatic Papers: Seaborn to Ottawa, undated.
30. NYT, pp.323-338; Gravel, Vol. Three, pp.289-290.
31. Gravel, Vol. Three, p.257.
32. Gravel, Vol. Three, p.290.
33. Confidential source.
34. Diplomatic Papers: Seaborn to Ottawa, Mar.5, 1965.
35. NYT, p.395.
36. Diplomatic Papers: Taylor to Rusk, Mar.7, 1965.
37. Diplomatic Papers: Taylor to Rusk, June 7, 1965.
38. Cooper, pp.432-433.
39. David Kraslow and Stuart H. Loory, *The Secret Search for Peace in Vietnam* (New York: Vintage Books, 1968), pp.15, 91-95.
40. NYT, pp.387-388.
41. Daniel Ellsberg, *Papers on the War* (New York: Pocket

Books, 1972), "The Quagmire Myth and the Stalemate Machine", pp.41-141.
42. NYT, pp.395-396.
43. Johnson, p.579. See also Kraslow and Loory, pp.97-109, and Cooper, pp.327-328, for a full discussion of this complicated and controversial incident.

THREE

1. Peter C. Dobell, *Canada's Search for New Roles* (Toronto: Oxford University Press, 1972), p.144.
2. Peter C. Newman, *The Distemper of Our Times* (Winnipeg: Greywood Publishing Limited, 1968), p.140.
3. Diplomatic Papers: Bundy to Lodge, Jan.27, 1966.
4. Martin to author.
5. Diplomatic Papers: Bundy to Butterworth; Butterworth to Bundy, Jan.28, 1966.
6. Diplomatic Papers: Butterworth to State Department, Jan.31, Feb.2, 1966.
7. Diplomatic Papers: State Department to US Embassy, Saigon, Feb.4, 1966.
8. Diplomatic Papers: Rusk to Martin, Feb.4, 1966.
9. Diplomatic Papers: Rice to Rusk, Feb.7, 1966.
10. Diplomatic Papers: Lodge to Rusk; Rusk to Lodge, Feb.25, 1966.
11. Diplomatic Papers: State Department to US Embassy, Saigon, Feb.24, 1966.
12. Diplomatic Papers: Lodge to Rusk, Mar.3, 1966.
13. This account of Ronning's first visit to Hanoi is based largely on two documents in the Diplomatic Papers: a cable to the State Department from the US Consulate-General in Hong Kong, Mar.15, 1966, and a State Department memorandum of a Washington meeting of Ronning, Bundy and other Canadian and US officials, Mar.20, 1966. See also Chester Ronning, *From the Boxer Rebellion to the People's Republic: A Memoir of China in*

Revolution (New York: Pantheon Books, 1974), Chap.16.

14. Ronning to author.
15. Martin to author.
16. Diplomatic Papers: State Department Memo, Apr.22, 1966; Butterworth to State Department, Apr.26, 1966.
17. Diplomatic Papers: Bundy to Rusk, Apr.22, 1966.
18. Diplomatic Papers: Memorandum to Government of Canada, Apr.26, 1966; Further Oral Message, Apr.30, 1966.
19. Diplomatic Papers: External Affairs cable, May 24, 1966.
20. Diplomatic Papers: Butterworth to Rusk, June 3, 1966; Lodge to Rusk, June 8, 1966.
21. NYT, pp.475-478.
22. Gravel, Vol. Four, p.104.
23. Martin to author.
24. Diplomatic Papers: US Embassy, Ottawa, to State Department, June 20, 1966.
25. Diplomatic Papers: Bundy to Rusk, Memorandum of Conversation, June 21, 1966; Dinner Meeting Memorandum, June 22, 1966. See also Ronning, Chap.16.
26. Martin to author.
27. Diplomatic Papers: State Department to US Embassy, Saigon, June 23, 1966.
28. NYT, pp.479-480.
29. Kraslow and Loory, Chaps.1-5; Cooper, pp.333-342.
30. Cooper, p.342.
31. Cooper, pp.372-374; Kraslow and Loory, pp.84-85.
32. James Steele, "Canada's Vietnam Policy: The Diplomacy of Escalation", in *An Independent Foreign Policy for Canada?*, ed. Stephen Clarkson (Toronto: McClelland and Stewart, 1968), p.74.
33. Walter Stewart, "Proudly We Stand the Butcher's Helper in Southeast Asia", *Maclean's*, March, 1970. See also John W. Warnock, *Partner to Behemoth, The Military Policy of a Satellite Canada* (Toronto: New Press, 1970), pp.246-251.

34. Warnock, p.249; *Toronto Star*, Nov.15, 1969; *The Globe and Mail*, Apr.28, 1971.
35. Kenneth McNaught, "From Colony to Satellite", in Clarkson, p.178.
36. Denis Smith, *Gentle Patriot: A Political Biography of Walter Gordon* (Edmonton: Hurtig Publishers, 1973), pp.322-325.
37. Martin to author; Gordon to author; Smith, p.325.
38. Martin to author.
39. Cooper, pp.330, 433.
40. Johnson, pp.233, 250, 255.
41. Cooper, p.382.
42. Kraslow and Loory, p.105n.
43. Martin to author.

FOUR

1. Dobell, p.11.
2. Bruce Thordarson, *Trudeau and Foreign Policy* (Toronto: Oxford University Press, 1972), p.66.
3: *Foreign Policy for Canadians* (Ottawa: Information Canada, 1970), p.23.
4. *Pacific* (Ottawa: Information Canada, 1970), p.24.
5. Thordarson, p.205.
6. Thomson and Swanson, p.118.
7. Mitchell Sharp, *Vietnam: Canada's Approach to Participation in the International Commission of Control and Supervision* (Ottawa: Information Canada, 1973), p.2.
8. John Best, "Vietnam Affair: Ottawa Gets a Lesson in How the US Doesn't Listen", *The Globe and Mail*, July 24, 1973.
9. The following section is based on interviews with several Ottawa sources.
10. Jacques Leslie in the *Los Angeles Times*, May 28, 1973.
11. Sharp, p.32.
12. John Swain of the London *Sunday Times*, in *The Globe and Mail*, July 25, 1973.

FIVE

1. Pearson, Vol. Two, p.183.
2. James Eayrs, "The Undefended Border", in *Canada — A Guide to the Peacable Kingdom*, ed. William Kilbourn (Toronto: Macmillan of Canada, 1970), p.215.
3. Eayrs, pp.216-217.
4. John W. Holmes, *The Better Part of Valour: Essays on Canadian Diplomacy* (Toronto: McClelland and Stewart, 1970), pp.51-52.
5. David Baldwin, "The Myths of the Special Relationship", in Clarkson, p.14.
6. Thomson and Swanson, p.131.
7. Holmes, p.172.

SELECTED BIBLIOGRAPHY

(A) THE UNITED STATES AND VIETNAM

Cooper, Chester L. *The Lost Crusade: America in Vietnam.* New York: Dodd Mead & Company, 1970.

Ellsberg, Daniel. *Papers on the War.* New York: Pocket Books, 1972.

FitzGerald, Frances. *Fire in the Lake: The Vietnamese and the Americans in Vietnam.* Boston: Little, Brown & Company, 1972.

Halberstam, David. *The Best and the Brightest.* Greenwich: Fawcett Publications, 1973.

Johnson, Lyndon Baines. *The Vantage Point: Perspectives of the Presidency, 1963-1969.* New York, Popular Library, 1971.

Kraslow, David and Stuart H. Loory. *The Secret Search for Peace in Vietnam.* New York: Vintage Books, 1968.

Lacouture, Jean. *Vietnam: Between Two Truces*. New York: Random House, 1966.

Raskin, Marcus G. and Bernard B. Fall, ed. *The Viet-Nam Reader*. New York: Vintage Books, 1967.

Shaplen, Robert. *The Lost Revolution*. New York: Harper & Row, 1965.

The Senator Gravel Edition. *The Pentagon Papers*. Four Volumes. Boston: Beacon Press, 1971.

The New York Times Edition. *The Pentagon Papers*. Written by Neil Sheehan, Hederick Smith, E. W. Kenworthy and Fox Butterfield. New York: Bantam Books, 1971.

Diplomatic Section. *The Pentagon Papers*. Unpublished.

(B) CANADA

Clarkson, Stephen, ed. *An Independent Foreign Policy for Canada?* Toronto: McClelland and Stewart, 1968.

Dobell, Peter C. *Canada's Search for New Roles: Foreign Policy in the Trudeau Era*. Toronto: Oxford University Press, 1972.

Gordon, J. King,, ed. *Canada's Role as a Middle Power*. Toronto: The Canadian Institute of International Affairs, 1966.

Holmes, John W. *The Better Part of Valour: Essays on Canadian Diplomacy*. Toronto: McClelland and Stewart, 1970.

Kilbourn, William, ed. *A Guide to the Peacable Kingdom*. Toronto: Macmillan of Canada, 1970.

Newman, Peter C. *Renegade in Power: The Diefenbaker Years*. Toronto: McClelland and Stewart, 1963.

Newman, Peter C. *The Distemper of Our Times*. Winnipeg: Greywood Publishing, 1968.

Pearson, Lester B. *Mike: The Memoirs of the Rt. Hon. Lester B. Pearson*. Volume One. 1897-1948. Toronto: University of Toronto Press, 1972.

Pearson, Lester B. *Mike: The Memoirs of the Rt. Hon. Lester*

B. Pearson. Volume Two. 1948-1957. ed. John A. Munro and Alex. I. Inglis. Toronto: University of Toronto Press, 1973.

Ronning, Chester. *From the Boxer Rebellion to the People's Republic: A Memoir of China in Revolution.* New York: Pantheon Books, 1974.

Smith, Denis. *Gentle Patriot: A Political Biography of Walter Gordon.* Edmonton: Hurtig Publishers, 1973.

Stewart, Walter. *Shrug: Trudeau in Power.* Toronto: New Press, 1971.

Thomson, Dale C. and Roger F. Swanson. *Canadian Foreign Policy: Options and Perspectives.* Toronto: McGraw-Hill Ryerson, 1971.

Thordarson, Bruce. *Trudeau and Foreign Policy: A Study in Decision Making.* Toronto: Oxford University Press, 1972.

Warnock, John W. *Partner to Behemoth: The Military Policy of a Satellite Canada.* Toronto: New Press, 1970.

Westell, Anthony. *Paradox: Trudeau as Prime Minister.* Scarborough: Prentice-Hall of Canada, 1972.

Masters, Donald C. *Canada in World Affairs: 1953 to 1955.* Toronto: Oxford University Press, 1959.

Eayrs, James. *Canada in World Affairs: October 1955 to June 1957.* Toronto: Oxford University Press, 1959.

Lloyd, Trevor. *Canada in World Affairs: 1957 to 1959.* Toronto: Oxford University Press, 1968.

Preston, Richard A. *Canada in World Affairs: 1959 to 1961.* Toronto: Oxford University Press, 1965.

Lyon, Peyton V. *Canada in World Affairs: 1961 to 1963.* Toronto: Oxford University Press, 1968.

(C) ESSAYS AND PAMPHLETS

Bauer, William E. "The Conflict in the Far East", in *The*

Communist States and the West, ed. Adam Bromke and Philip E. Uren. New York: Frederick A. Praeger, 1967.

Bridle, Paul. *Canada and the International Commissions in Indochina, 1954-1972.* Toronto: The Canadian Institute of International Affairs, 1973.

Holmes, John. "Canada and the Vietnam War", in *War and Society in North America.* ed. J. L. Granatstein and R. D. Cuff. Toronto: Thomas Nelson and Sons, 1971.

Martin, Paul. *Canada and the Quest for Peace.* Toronto: The Copp Clark Publishing Company, 1967.

Sharp, Mitchell. *Vietnam: Canada's Approach to Participation in the International Commission of Control and Supervision, October 25, 1972-March 27, 1973.* Ottawa: Information Canada, 1973.

A Foreign Policy for Canadians. Six pamphlets. Ottawa: Information Canada, 1970.

Viet-Nam: What Kind of Peace: Documents and Analysis of the 1973 Paris Agreement on Viet-Nam. Washington: Indochina Resource Center, 1973.

INDEX

Donahue, Major Jerry: 107
Dong, Pham Van: 3, 59-61, 67-8, 70, 76, 84, 103-4, 106, 109, 111, 128, 130
Dulles, John Foster: 3, 12, 35, 186

Eden, Anthony: 3, 5
Ellsberg, Daniel: 21, 79

Gandhi, Indira: 116
Gauvin, Michel: 159-74, 178-9
Geneva Agreements: 3, 5, 8, 11, 16, 18, 20, 24, 29, 33, 38, 111
Geneva Conference (on Indochina — 1954): vi, 12, 32, 59, 70
Geneva Conference (on Laos — 1962): 31
Gillespie, Alastair: 175
Goldwater, Barry: 68
Gordon, Walter: ix, 124-6
Green, Howard: iv, 24-6
Gromyko, Andrei: 117

Harriman, Averell: 57, 69, 119
Head, Ivan: ix, 140, 145, 154-7
Ho Chi Minh: 3, 12, 47-8, 50, 81, 92, 95, 102
Hungary: vi, 144, 148, 151, 159-62, 164-6, 169-74, 176

India: v, 8, 19-20, 24, 30, 35
Indonesia: vi, 144, 148, 151, 171-4
International Commission of Control and Supervision: vi, 23-4, 30, 151-5, 158-82, 187, 194
International Control Commission (in Cambodia): 5, 30-2

International Control Commission (in Laos): 5, 30-1
International Control Commission (in Vietnam): v-vi, 5-45, 82, 84, 117-9, 143-6, 152, 157-9, 163, 174

Johnson, Lyndon: 23, 27, 38, 40, 48-50, 52-5, 57, 60, 63-5, 68, 71-2, 74, 77, 79-85, 91-2, 108, 116, 118, 127-9, 182-3, 187-8

Kennedy, John F.: 79-80
Kennedy, Robert: 127
Ketcheson, Donald: 18
Khanh, Gen. Nguyen: 26, 62, 64
King, William Lyon Mackenzie: 186
Kissinger, Henry: 140, 144-5, 147, 151, 154-7, 165, 172, 176-7, 179, 182

Lansdale, Col. Edward G.: 13
La Pira, Giorgio: 91
Lau, Col. Ha Van: 70, 73, 107
Laviolette, Capt. Charles: 169
Leger, Jules: 22
Lewandowski, Janusz: 117
Lodge, Henry Cabot: 43, 47, 49, 51-3, 55, 57, 59, 81, 95, 97, 99, 101, 108, 110, 113, 117

McCarthy, Eugene: 127
Macdonald, Donald: 140, 175
McNamara, Robert: 21, 37, 49, 75, 108, 110
Marchand, Jean: 140
Marr, Dr. David G.: 18
Martin, Paul: ix, 18, 22, 26-7, 29, 34-40, 46-7, 50-2, 55, 58, 66, 83-5, 87, 92-8, 100,

209

Date Due

March 12			

DISCARDED